TUTORING:
Complete Home
Business Guide

Kimberly Davison-Fujioka

DEDICATION

To the teacher within all of us.

To teach, according to Freire is

"...to begin always anew, to make, to reconstruct, and not to spoil, to refuse to bureaucratize the mind, to understand and to live life as a process--live to become..." Paulo Freire

ISBN-10: 1463566239
ISBN-13: 978-1463566234

Introduction

I wrote this book for people who want to succeed at building a home tutoring business. I tutored in my home for over twenty years. During this time, I lived in various cities in the U.S. and in Japan due to my husband's work. Therefore, I needed a job where I could earn money quickly and reliably in a new location. To my surprise, tutoring was in demand everywhere I lived. In addition, I discovered that I could earn more money than I ever thought possible by tutoring online, where I could invite many students to join one live session.

This book contains two parts: the business side and the teaching or tutoring side. By reading this book you will learn both. The first part of this book focuses on the business aspects of the tutoring field: how to set up your business and how to get tutoring referral agencies to refer students to you.

In this book, I tell you how to advertise for free and how to keep students coming back for more lessons.

In addition, I teach you how to tutor in a face-to-face traditional tutoring situation and online. There are two detailed chapters on tutoring online—how to set up your business, how to execute a lesson and what hardware and online messaging systems to use. In addition, I list a few inexpensive webcams. In the appendix, I list websites where you are free to advertise your online tutoring services.

There is no book like this for sale in the bookstores. Most of the teaching books instruct readers on how to teach in a classroom situation. Only a few books specify the tutoring field, and none detail step-by-step how to set up your business with up-to-date-links to online resources. These online resources exist now. You can start tutoring immediately after you receive this book.

In my career as an English Instructor, I have taught hundreds of students from all over the world to speak English. I have taught in classrooms and I have tutored students individually. I have also taught in small groups of four to six students. I have a Masters degree in Applied Linguistics (TESL), Teaching English as a Second Language. I taught English at universities all over the world from 1982 until recently when I left teaching to focus on my writing. I taught at University of California at Berkeley, UC Davis and several universities in Japan, Saitama University, Gunma University and Gunma Prefectural Women's University. (I lived in Japan for six years.) I have also tutored privately for as many years as I taught at the university level.

Everything I share with you in this book I have done. I am sharing it with you, so you can do it too.

Tutoring is a very rewarding job. You can really change the lives of the students you tutor.

Sincerely,

Kimberly Davison-Fujioka

Visit me at my website where you can read some chapter excerpts and purchase the ebook in PDF for only $9.99.

http://www.tutoringasuccessfulbusiness.com

Table of Contents

Part I Tutoring as a Business

Part II Tutoring International People Whose First Language is not English

ACKNOWLEDGMENTS

I want to acknowledge the professors I studied under at the University of Surrey and to all the students who I have tutored. Now after 25 years of teaching and tutoring, I can offer you my experience and advice.

Most of all, I want to thank my spouse, Kazutoshi Fujioka and my son, Kazuumi.

Chapter 1

"Tutoring and Test Preparation is Booming,"
according to the U.S. Industry Report.

"With the recession in full effect, unemployed Americans began returning to school at an increasing rate, boosting demand for tutoring and test preparation services. While this trend is expected to continue, other factors will contribute to the industry's forecast growth." **May 20, 2010, U.S. Industry Report**.

Amazingly, tutors are earning more than ever and while most Americans have little money to spend, they are using it for tutoring either for themselves or their children.

Even the Gifted are Turning to Tutors

According to the Chicago Tribune, "even the gifted are now turning to tutors". A reporter from the Chicago Tribune stated that, "Today, though, tutoring has evolved way beyond the remedial to a form of instruction for top-level students as well as those as young as kindergartners. It's a twist that says a lot about academic anxiety among some Americans, competitive parents and a rising gap in what experts call educational equity."

Why are so many people seeking tutors?

The answer is simple. It is a fact that everyone knows:

More education means more earning power.

Parents are choosing a better life for their children when they invest in tutoring and, after that, higher education. As a result, tutors are in demand. When demand increases prices go up, as we all know. As a result, people who tutor can ask for even more money for their services.

I never tutor for less than $40.00 per hour; and I often receive $100.00 per hour by scheduling several students with similar learning goals at the same meeting.

Their parents pay ahead of time for their sessions, each one pays $25.00 per hour for group tutoring sessions. Do the math and you can see how easily you can earn good money in the tutoring business.

This is an excellent time to start a tutoring business!

Chapter 2

Tutoring in Your Home vs Regular Employment

You might be asking yourself, is tutoring for me? Let's examine the differences between working part-time at a regular job or working for yourself as a tutor.

The list below compares the benefits between tutoring and regular part-time or full-time employment.

Operate Your Own Tutoring Business

•Start your business in a few days

•Tutor as many as hours you want

•Choose your own hours

•Earn between $40 and $100 per hour

•Build relationships with parent/clients and feel appreciated

•Tutor the same students who appreciate your knowledge

•Tax savings on all business related expenses

•Work in your own home, public library or coffee shop

•Stay home with your children

or

Working as a Part-time or Full-time Employee

•Spend weeks searching for a job

•Work when the employer needs you which means weekends and holidays

•Receive a weekly schedule

•Earn an hourly wage set by the employer $12.00 to $15.00 per hour

•Wait on customers and stand on your feet all day long or sit at a desk in one position all day

•Feel unappreciated

•Drive to the workplace in traffic and then back home again

•Hire a babysitter, ask friends to be with your children or leave them at home

It is obvious when comparing the lists that working for yourself is better than working for someone else.

What kind of person would be good at tutoring?

Take the self –assessment quiz to see if tutoring is a good fit for you.

Self-Assessment Quiz

Take the simple Self-Assessment Quiz to find out if tutoring is for you. Answer yes or no. (Yes means that the statement describes you while no means it doesn't.)

Part I

When I work at a regular job, for someone else, I watch the clock.

I often feel like I am wasting my time at work.

At a regular job, I follow instructions but I have a better way of doing it.

Part II

When I set my mind to doing something, I usually do it.

I do not have trouble motivating myself when I decide to do something.

I set goals for myself and follow through achieving them.

When I have several jobs to do, I can decide which one has to be done first.

I can break down a complex job into smaller parts.

Part III

I feel good when I help people.

I like showing people how to do things.

I like to interact with different kinds of people.

I like to help people feel good about themselves.

I like to solve people's problems.

People usually like me.

I like variety in my work.

Answers: There are no correct answers, only responses that will help you determine if working as a tutor fits your personality.

The first 3 questions reflect your discontent in working for other people. If you answered yes to most of these you probably would be happier working for yourself.

The second set of questions measure your ability to motivate yourself which is a pre-requisite for working for yourself. If you answered yes for most of these then working for yourself is good for you.

The third set of questions relate to working with people, in a teaching situation, especially tutoring. If you answered yes to most of these questions, then tutoring is a good job for you.

Congratulations!

You now know yourself better and can decide if working for yourself or tutoring is a good fit for you.

Chapter 3

Defining Your Goals

Is this your first time starting a business? If this is your first business venture, then you need to read this chapter. Because in order to succeed, you need to have a plan; and before you make a plan you must define your goals.

By understanding the information in this ebook and taking action, you can achieve great success.

But first you must do one thing: clarify or define your goals. After you define your goals, you can make a plan.

Define Your Goals.

Success can be defined as achieving your goals. In order to measure success, you must have clear and precise goals.

So my question to you is:

What are your goals?

Do you want to:

Spend more time with your family?

Retire without spending all of your money in the bank?

Make an extra $200 to $500 per week?

Experience what it's like to make money and be your own boss?

Help students feel good about themselves?

Be truly appreciated for your service?

Go full time with your tutoring business?

Tutor part-time while taking college courses?

Tutor part-time and play golf for the rest of the day?

What do you want to achieve by having your own tutoring business?

Only you can decide. Once you decide on your goals, your mind will be clear about how to use your time.

You can expect that your tutoring service will make a tremendous difference in both parents and students lives but what is more critical is that it have importance to your life.

Do you want to tutor? Do you enjoy it?

Fill in your answers under the questions:

Defining Your Goals as a Tutor

How much time do you have to devote to tutoring?

If you have children, what hours of the day can you tutor?

How much money do you want to make?

Do you want to have students in your home?

What facilities exist in your community where you can meet students?

What subjects interest you?

What did you excel at in school?

What subjects do you enjoy reading?

What age children do you like most?

Are there specific ages of children that you feel more comfortable with?

How will you handle a student who is not motivated to study?

How will you interact with parents?

Will you drive to a student's home? If so, will you charge more?

Will your lessons be the typical one hour?

Will you combine lessons into small groups, by arranging students to meet together?

How many students will you see at one time?

How will you handle a student not showing up for their appointment?

After you answer these questions, your answers can guide your overall tutoring plan. Your plan will be comprised of your answers to these questions. Your plan will detail how you will run your tutoring business; it will be in line with your specific goals.

Are you like Roberta?

Roberta is a mother of three who are all in school. She only has 12 hours a week to dedicate to tutoring, from 3pm until 6pm, M-F because she wants to be at home with her family after 6pm on the weekdays and on the weekends. Her plan was only to accept students who could see her between 3 and 6pm M-F. Therefore, when she listed her tutoring services with a referral provider, she stated 3pm-6pm M-F. In addition, she wanted to earn about $1,900 a month. She decided to only accept long term students who needed to come several times a week. She charged $40.00 per hour for each hour of tutoring. Roberta was quite busy between 3 and 6pm but more than a typical day's wages during those three hours.

Your goals and business plan will be made clear to parents on your contact sheet where you describe your policies and prices.

Hand it out to parents or adult students at the first meeting.

The next page "Contact Sheet Contents" outlines what should be on the contact sheet.

Contact Sheet Contents

Your tutoring business name (ex., Kim's Tutoring)

Hours available: 2:30 pm to 7pm M-F, Sat 10am to 3pm Sun. Not available.

Subjects tutored: Here you select the areas you choose to tutor. For example, Language Arts. Language Arts refers to reading and English related subject areas such as writing and grammar. Social Studies is another area. Social Studies means history and sociology as well as geography and cultures. Art. Art is drawing and painting as well as other arts like pottery or jewelry making. Math. Math includes basic mathematics and algebra, geometry and statistics. ESL (English as a Second Language). ESL is another subject area which refers to tutoring students from other countries who want to learn how to speak English. Some of them may also want to learn how to read and write.

Grades tutored: Here you select the grade levels you want to work with, for example, elementary students (ages 6-12), middle school students (ages12 –14) or high school students (ages14-18). In addition, you can add college students. Adults is another category of learners you may want to tutor. For example, adults who are new immigrants may want to learn English speaking or writing.

Rates: Here is where you state the rates that you choose. Check the ads in your city newspaper or craigslist.org to check the average tutoring rates in your geographic area. I charge $40.00 per hour for individual tutoring sessions of one hour. If the lesson goes over one hour, in order to cover a special topic, the charges are $15.00 for 15 minutes after one hour.

(I charge $25.00 per hour for group sessions. Groups are no larger than six students and most groups are only four students. Groups are usually better because you can earn more but also the students get a better rate; and after they meet each other they may want to study together between sessions. You can put an ad on craigslist and ask them to sign up for small classes. You can put your ad in the community section under classes. In addition, you can put your tutoring ad in the tutoring section under services.

Make sure to advertise for your classes a few weeks ahead of time, so people have time to see your ad and sign up. In addition, you can put your ad up other places like the library or at the schools.)

Tutoring Sessions: This is where you state whether you will teach one-to-one as in individual sessions or to a group of students. You can state Individual or Group, or both Individual & Group

Describe: In this section you describe the types of tutoring sessions you offer, individual lessons are one full hour. Group lessons are one full hour with 4-6 students.

Location: In this section, you describe where you are willing to tutor. Will you tutor at your home or at the student's home? At a public library or a coffee shop? Some people tutor at a mall in their area. In the public spaces of a mall there are often places with chairs where people congregate. In addition, often times the public school is open in the afternoon, after classes are over. They offer after school classes, sports activities or club meetings. You can ask the secretary if you could meet students there. In addition, at college campuses there are many free public spaces where you can meet a student. Keep in mind when choosing a place, that it has easy access to a restroom. In addition, notice the hours it is open, especially if it's a library.

Late policy: Here is where you state your late policy. If the student is late to class, the time will not be extended. (This is a courtesy to the next student coming next.)

If the student is late to a group tutoring session, he or she will have to catch up on their own without disrupting the class.

Cancellation Policy: Here is where you explain your cancellation policy. I state that cancellation must be 24 hours in advance. If not, the fee cannot be refunded. Of course if the student becomes ill, for example at school that day, and the parent calls you, that is an exception.

Discipline Policy: Here is where you explain your discipline policy.

The student brings his computer game to the lesson and keeps touching it or looking for it in his backpack and, basically, not paying attention.

> My policy for computer game players and other electronic gadgets is that they will be confiscated. When the student sits down at the lesson, I hold out my hand and say,

21

"Give me your gameboy." I take the game player and sit it on the table on the other side of me until the lesson is over. When the lesson is over, he gets it back.

The student keeps getting phone calls on her cell phone during the lesson. The same policy as for the gameboy. If the student is older she or he can turn their phone off and hold their own phone.

The student's friends appear at the lesson, if it's a coffee shop or library. They try to talk to the student or tease the student. They disrupt the lesson.

The policy for this issue is: the student's friends cannot interrupt the lesson. If they attempt to, I intercede and tell them to sit quietly somewhere else.

The student does not do their homework. (This can become a recurrent issue. The way to handle this issue is critical to being a successful tutor with children or young adults.)

The most important thing to remember is this student is coming to tutoring because, obviously, they are not doing well in school.

And why is that?

(You will discover one interpretation at the initial interview with the parent or parents. However, if you experience discipline problems during the tutoring sessions you can begin to understand why the student is not doing well in school.)

One reason why students do not do well in school is because they are not doing their homework.

They do not do their homework because they do not know how. They need extra help from a tutor so they can understand the lesson and carry out the homework assignment.

Another reason they are not doing their homework is because they are choosing to play or waste time in some other way.

The tutor must get to the root of the problem of why they are not doing their homework.

If they need to review the concepts that the teacher covered in school before they do their homework, then the tutor can do that—clarify the principles that were taught in the school lesson(s).

If they need to learn to organize their time and be accountable for their work, the tutor can help them with that by assigning them work in front of the tutor. The tutor waits while the student performs the task, then rewards him or her for their work.

The tutor needs to do this regularly. The reason for this is to build up their study skills, step by step.

In addition, the tutor needs to assign homework outside of the lesson and clearly state what they want to see from the student for the next session.

For example, I have an algebra student who comes three days a week. I go over a type of simple equation with him, showing him, step-by-step how to do it. Before he leaves the tutoring session that day, I give him 5 problems as homework. For the next lesson, he will have to bring with him that homework which shows me that he can do that type of equation.

Finally, concerning homework, if the student repeatedly does not do their homework, I discuss it with the parents to get their support. The parent(s) usually promise to discipline the student at home to make sure they do their homework.

After you complete the contact sheet you hand it out to your students at the first lesson.

Chapter 4

Deciding What Subjects to Tutor

The most popular subject students need help in is Math. If you can tutor Algebra or higher, you'll put yourself in a great position to attract many students and maintain monthly students that will guarantee you paychecks each and every month.

Algebra isn't the only subject in demand by parents and students.

Other subjects parents actively hire tutors for include:

English/or ESL(English as a Second Language)

Writing

Reading

Foreign languages

History

Science

Chemistry

Biology

Basic Math

Statistics

Trigonometry

Calculus

Music, such as, an instrument

Tutor in the subject that is the easiest for you. If you have been out of school for awhile and have forgotten the subject areas, go to the library and do a little reading.

The book series called "What your ___grader Needs to Know" by Hirsch is a good reference. Some of the exact titles are "What your Fourth Grader Needs to Know" by Hirsch; What your Sixth Grader Needs to Know; What your Tenth Grader Needs to Know etc. These books outline the typical subject areas for specific grade levels.

Don't be intimidated by the subject area because it is quite easy and after you start reading the material, it will all come back to you. As soon as you open up one of these books, you'll realize how much you already know.

For the tutoring session, you won't be expected to provide your own textbooks. The student will want you to use their textbooks to help them. However, having said that, I suggest that for the first session you have a few books sitting on your desk or table beside you. If the student hasn't brought their textbook and you run out of things to talk about, you can always open up a textbook, find a quiz and give it to the student. Or if the student needs tutoring in reading, you can ask him or her to read a passage aloud.

Test Preparation

Test preparation is another area for tutoring. Some of the tests that students study for are as follows:

1.SSAT: Pre college entrance exam/ exam for private school entrance

The SSAT measures the student's grade level knowledge in comparison with other students in their same grade across the U.S. It is a tool used for private school entry and placement. It is taught according to level: elementary, middle school or high school. There are test preparation books available that you can purchase or borrow from the library to help you tutor a student.

2.SAT: College Entrance Exam

When you tutor students for the SAT you will go over practice tests as well as types of questions and answers that will be on the exam. The best way is to purchase a SAT test taking book because they contain SAT practice tests, including with new recent exams. You will help the student become familiar with the math, critical reading, and writing sections of the SAT. In addition, you will help them read the practice essay questions and the sample essays. You will provide a review of the math concepts tested in the exam. You will teach them test-taking approaches and suggestions that underscore important points.

3.TOFEL: English speaking and listening exam for international people

The TOFEL Exam measures the abilities of international people in listening, speaking, reading and writing in English. This exam is relatively easy to teach for a native speaker for English. It requires an audio player like a CD player or laptop computer with a DVD/CD player. The study guides available for teaching usually have a CD and they have many practice tests as well as rudimentary materials in grammar, idioms or slang and conversational speaking.

4.GED: Test for High School Diploma

The GED is an easy exam to tutor, since it measures what students have to know for high school graduation. In the public library you can find a book on what is covered in the GED. If your student needs GED tutoring, take the book out of the library and use that as a template for what to teach the student.

5.GRE: The Graduate Record Exam.

This is the test for Graduate School. It is specified in each subject area. For example, there is one for English Literature. This exam measures a student's knowledge of English and literature college level courses, to determine their readiness for graduate school. A student would take this exam prior to applying to enter a Master's or PhD program. In order to be competent to tutor students for this test, you need to have a graduate degree in the specific area. For example, if you want to tutor for the GRE in Mathematics you should already have a Master's degree or PhD in that subject area. This is an appropriate test for graduate students to tutor undergraduates who want to attend university at the graduate level.

Tutoring for these tests require many tutoring sessions. Students can be pre-billed for these tutorials as a group.

You might be asking yourself: why do the students need a tutor if they can use the test preparation book?

They need you to be there to motivate them and help them along the way. In a sense, tutoring for test preparation involves a lot of encouraging and hand holding.

Music

Tutoring in a musical instrument is another area. Can you play the piano? Flute? Clarinet? If you can play an instrument, then you can tutor students in that instrument. Go to the local schools and talk to the music teacher or band teacher. Give them your business card. In addition, go to the music stores and tack up your card on the bulletin board. Introduce yourself to the manager of the store and give her your business card. Music stores are inundated with instrument tutoring requests from parents.

Chapter 5

Develop Your Tutoring Business with These Six Tools

In order to build a success tutoring business, it's important to apply these six tools. Utilizing these tools will help your business get off to a fast start.

1. Create a Tutoring-type Email Address.

To look professional, you'll need to communicate with a professional email name that has something to do with your online tutoring business. For example, "JohnBrownsonlinetutoring@yahoo.com." This can be done by going to https://login.yahoo.com/config/mail and setting up your email at yahoo.com.

2. Print Your Business Cards. Business cards are key to getting your online tutoring business started. When people ask, "What do you do?" you can hand them a business card and tell them you own a tutoring business.

By going to http://www.vistaprint.com, you can get 250 free business cards and choose from 100's of designs. You'll have to pay for shipping, less than $5.00, but this is still a great deal!

They also have other items like signs and brochures that I have used. For example, they have a heavy weight sign, covered with glossy cardboard that you can buy for less than $20.00 and put on the front of your house or apt, or on the back window of your car. Any of their designs on the website can be made into a sign or business card. All you have to do is type in your own information into their form, like your name, phone number and email address and/or website address.

I put my tutoring sign in the back window of my car. People come up to me all the time at the grocery store to ask about tutoring.

3. Offer a Toll-free 800# for Potential Clients to Call

http://ww.best800service.com offers a free trial and packages start at $9.95 per month. You can instantly point your 800 number to your cell or home phone, and you can set up a messaging system and view all incoming calls. Be sure to put your 800 number on your business cards.

4. Sign Up For a Merchant Account

You don't need to spend hundreds of dollars to set up a merchant account. Just go to http://ww.paypal.com and create a free account. You can upgrade the account and receive your own virtual terminal. This will allow you to process your client's credit or debit cards, and accepts MasterCard, Visa, Discover and American Express. The money you collect will be deposited directly into your bank account.

5. Make an ad to put on Craigslist. www.craigslist.org

Your ad needs to include a few points: The name of your tutoring ad with your name and the subjects you tutor, as well as characteristics about your tutoring style that would attract a parent, like "kind and caring" and/or "motivates your child to learn" In addition, you can say something about your own educational background, high school graduate, honors student, mother with children of her own, college student etc.

6. Make signs to put around at various locations, such as, the public library, near a school, at the grocery store, at the laundry mat, at a university library or at coffee shops. The sign should have these important facts: 1. The name of your tutoring business, like Kim's Tutoring 2. The names of the subjects you tutor. 3. The locations where you will travel, like the public library or coffee shop or the student's home or have students come to your home. 4. Your phone number and or email address. 5. Announce a one time free tutoring session.

Tips: Make a template sign and put little stickers around it to make it appear attractive. I went to the local craft store and purchased a couple of those scrap booking stickers of pencils, apples and a little school house. Then I positioned those on my tutoring sign, so it looks appealing. I make color copies of that template which I post everywhere.

In addition, I taped a few business cards to the bottom of my sign, so parents can just take one of the business cards.

Chapter 6

Deciding Your Hourly Rate

When tutoring, you can charge as much or as little as you want. If you look at the competition, you'll see some tutors charge as little as $25.00 per hour while some charge more than $50.00 per hour.

In addition, if you decide to teach test preparation classes you can tutor several students at one time, using a room at the local public library or university library. You can easily charge each student only $25.00 per session and still make $100.00 to $200.00 for each one hour session. (You can find test preparation books at the library, which you can use to teach the group.)

I recommend you do a search on craigslist to see how much other tutors in your city are charging. (Don't undercut the other tutor's prices. Just charge the same price so you don't seem too pricey. After you tutor in the area and people get to know you, raise your rates a little.) If you don't have a craigslist in your city, then check the local newspaper or bulletin boards for other tutor's ads.

Most tutors offer curriculum based tutoring. That means that they tutor students in a specific grade, a specific subject. For example, 7th grade students who are taking pre algebra; and they tutor according to the public or private school curriculum. (You might be asking yourself, "How do I find out the school curriculum? You can go to a local schools and talk to the librarian. She will have the names of the books they are using. In addition, you may want to meet with the guidance counselor. She can be a great resource because she knows all the students who need extra help. You can give her a few of your business cards when you meet with her.)Some tutors offer a special kind of help. They tutor students who need remedial work such as in reading, writing, math or ESL, speaking English.

(Remedial work means that the student cannot perform at the grade level they are in; they need more background.)

Remedial Tutoring: If a student comes to me and is reading at the third grade level but they are in the fifth grade, then I know they need remedial work. I give them third grade reading tasks and help them improve until they achieve their grade level.

Since you're starting your own tutoring business, you can choose what is going to make you unique.

If you want to focus on Language Arts then you can tutor in reading and writing. If you want to focus on Math then you can tutor in basic math, algebra and geometry. If you want to focus on SPED special education then you can work only in that area.

If you want to be unique in the marketplace and charge a high hourly rate, all you have to do is take the time to care by consulting with your clients (the parents).

You can confidently charge between $40.00 - $50.00 per hour depending on the location of your client and the specialty. For example, test prep usually pays more per hour.

The pricing options you decide on must pi discounts for more monthly hours. Here are examples. (Each lesson is one hour)

1 lesson and up to 3 lessons or hours per week $119 per week ($40 per hour)

4 lessons and up to 6 lessons or hours per week $199 per week ($32.50 per hour)

7 lessons and up to10 lessons or hours per week for $249 per week ($25.00 per hour)

Parents will usually choose your most discounted offer even if the monthly price is higher. If your students need extra hours, charge them the same amount they are paying with your plan. Don't give extra discounts.

Chapter 7

Tutor Online to Earn More Money

Tutoring online is very different than tutoring in person. You need to decide if you want to tutor online. Online tutoring consists of sitting at your computer talking into a small camera with audio, to another person who is doing the same. You have to speak clearly and rely only on your facial expressions for nonverbal communication.

Person-to-person tutoring is more personal. You get to see the student and get to know them on a personal level. On the other hand, online is more profitable and you can meet people from all over the world. In the long run, it is better to learn online tutoring because it is the way of the future especially for teaching ESL(English as a Second Language). Technology is getting better and better making it easier to do it. For example, Skype can now come through your tv screen. What this means for tutoring is that you can see multiple students, at the same time, during an online class.(In this book, I will not teach you how to do that because I don't have the type of TV for Skype, so I don't know how to do it yet. You can get onto Skype's website to find out.)

When you tutor online you must insist they pay first, using Paypal before you tutor. (Of course you can give them the first introductory lesson for free before they decide. But don't teach for an entire hour, only 15 minutes.) In online tutoring, the least you can earn is $10.00 to $15.00 per 15 minutes. You can also tutor many students at the same time, so the earning potential is much higher.

Tutoring Online Requires Some Computer Knowledge

Tutoring Online requires computer knowledge. In short, you must learn the specifics of using the webcam and how to teach using a webcam. When you buy a webcam, the directions will be provided. It isn't difficult.

When you begin using the webcam, you must look directly into the video and speak clearly while limiting your expressions to your face and upper body. I practiced this with my husband before doing it with a student.

Since the webcam sits on the top of your computer, it has to be adjusted according to your height. I suggest you use a webcam with a built in audio because it's easier. However, if you choose a separate audio you will wear a headset with a microphone attached that you will speak into.

When you buy the webcam it is best to buy the headset as a bundle so that you know they work well together. However, if you buy the webcam with the built in audio then you know it works together.

The beauty of using the webcam is that you can do it almost anywhere. You can do it in a coffee shop from your own laptop computer, with an online connection and a microphone and small video camera.

Good Webcam Choices for Low Price to Mid Priced (Microphone/Video combinations for online tutoring):

Logitech Webcam 250 $39.99

This webcam is a low price but very good quality. It requires your computer OS to be Windows XP or higher. The details are listed below.
Windows® XP (SP2 or higher)
1GHz, RAM(512 MB)
Windows Vista® or Windows® 7 (32-bit or 64-bit)
1 GHz
512 MB Ram
200 MB Hard drive space
CD Rom Drive

The Specs for this webcam are listed below.
Enhanced VGA sensor, Video Capture 800 by 600 pixels
Photos: up to 1.3 megapixels, 30 frames per second.
Built in microphone with Right sound technology
The Logitech webcam software will allow you to do as follows:
Make a Logitech Video, capture videos and make and view photos
Email videos and photos
Use and upload YouTube
Works with Skype, Windows Live Messenger, AOL Instant Messenger and other applications.

Face Vision Touch Cam N1 $119.00, V1 model $70.00

The FV TouchCam N1 does high definition video at 720p and is compatible with any version of Windows from XP and on up. It has high speed and a USB 2.0

to connect to the computer. It has 720 video calling even when the other person you are calling does not have the same equipment. You can make videos and quick photos as well as take part in video conferencing.

Specs:

HD 720p video calls

H.264 Adaptive H264 encoder for great video experience.

Wide angle lens with 78 degrees.

Dual microphones with unidirectional support beam forming technology for great audio performance.

Auto focus: images are sharp even close-ups are sharp.

USB interface with true plug and play experience.

Skype certified.

Face Vision Webcam N1 $119.00, Face Vision V1 $70.00

Philips Webcam

Philips Webcam SPZ6500
$79.99

The Philips Webcam SPZ6500

The Philips Webcam has 2.0 Mega Pixels. The number of mega pixels is key to determining the image quality. The 2.0 Mega Pixels CMOS sensor provides high quality video images not usually associated with webcams.

Two microphones. Your voice can be heard naturally in clear stereo sound. Dual built-in directional microphones and Philips-patented audio beaming technology create a virtual noise and echo-free zone.

Only the voice of the user is captured, with other sounds minimized.

After deciding what webcam to use, you can choose the audio video communication system or messaging system you want to use for tutoring, such as, Skype.

There are many options available and many are even free. I will highlight some below. Check out their websites because they provided step by step instructions on how to set it up on your computer and how to use it. They have support services for extra help too.

Online Teleconferencing Systems using both Audio and Video

Skype--www.skype.com

Features: Skype allows you to make conference calls. You can video and audio call many people at the same time. In addition, you can do screen sharing. All of the people you are communicating with through your conference call can see your power point presentation on their computer screen. Skype allows you to make one-on-one video calls. Through Skype you can tutor individually or a group of students. Skype is free.

How to Use Skype

Equipment for Using Skype

The items you will need are: a computer that is on-line (the faster the internet connection the better), a web camera and microphone, either built into the computer or an external plug-in one, preferably a headset with a microphone.

Download Skype

Go to Skype website and download the software. Click the download icon and then, on the left side, click "download now". Next, click "run" and install.

Make a Skype Account

You need to create a Skype Account. It is free. You can click on getting started, or click on "don't have a Skype name." A window will open where you can to create an account. You register easily by adding your name, email, a password, and a user name.

Add your Contacts/Students

You can search for students who have registered with Skype. Type their full name in the search bar. Then click on the correct city, click to add the contact and type a short message to tell your student to add you as a contact.

Make a Free Video Calls

Click the green video call button. You can answer with the video button. If you are not able to hear the person during the video conference call, check the volume of your speaker. On the other hand, if they are not able to hear you, check your microphone. Make sure it is plugged into your computer.

Hardware Requirements:

Your computer should have 1 Ghz processor or faster.

You need to have 256 MB of RAM with 100 MG of free disk space on your hard drive.

You need a webcam, a microphone and speakers or a headset. The best is to get a webcam with a built in microphone.

Vyew---www.vyew.com

Vyew is an excellent system for tutoring. You can easily create and upload course content to use during real-time teaching and for anytime use. Students can get on and use it together for learning or they can get on alone too access lesson material.

Educators

You can teach one person or an online classroom teaching multiple students in real-time.

Using Vyew you can post course syllabuses and worksheets for students to review and to work on together.

Tutors

Students can review their lessons and post questions even when you're not available

Students

Work on group projects together, outline responsibilities, contribute to the class lesson.

Post group project files in Vyew's File Storage to ensure everyone has access to the latest version.

With Vyew, online meeting places or rooms can be opened indefinitely, Instructors can allow students to come in at their convenience.

Vyew provides a multi-modal environment for education and training. Almost any content can be uploaded to or created in Vyew for a rich, interactive environment that includes interactive Flash learning objects, audio, video, graphics, presentations, spreadsheets and text.

Equipment: The items you will need are: a computer that is on-line (the faster the internet connection the better), a web camera and microphone, either built into the computer or an external plug-in one, preferably a headset with a microphone.

Hardware System Requirements:

Your computer should have 1 Ghz processor or faster.

You need to have 256 MB of RAM.

You need a webcam, a microphone and speakers or a headset. The best is to get a webcam with a built in microphone.

Edu 2.0---www.edu20.org

This system is designed for educators. It is great! You get your own school website where you can easily see a list of your students, the classes you are teaching as well as any other information such as lessons/presentations that you will give to your students. You interact with students during the classes and keep track of all your online materials in one place. There is a calendar feature integrated with your courses as well as many other useful features. It is free but the more advanced features cost $4.95 per month. When you register you get all of the features including the advanced ones for free for 30 days.

Equipment: The items you will need are: a computer that is on-line (the faster the internet connection the better), a web camera and microphone, either built into the computer or an external plug-in one, preferably a headset with a microphone.

System Requirements: Your computer should have 1 Ghz processor or faster.

You need to have 256 MB of RAM.

You need a webcam, a microphone and speakers or a headset. The best is to get a webcam with a built in microphone.

With one or more of the audio video communication systems listed above used at the same time, you can conduct online tutoring sessions with your students and make great money for your services.

You can read about each online tutoring software at their websites. As you'll see, they are all free but some have advanced features that cost a low fee. Keep in mind that you can use two or more at the same time.

You can make a video for utube as a way to advertise your online tutoring services. In addition, you can use that same video on Craigslist, ebay classifieds, yahoo classifieds and other free advertising spaces.

Chapter 8

The Virtual Classroom for Online Tutoring

The virtual classroom differs from the regular classroom mainly by the methods of communication. Instead of in-person, you are online. The tools are: the microphone and audio as well as the computer, and the white board or online place where you display lesson materials. Get a good headset and become familiar with using the whiteboard.

Practice using it with a friend or your partner, so you have it mastered before you actually begin using it with a student or students.

The virtual classroom relies on a microphone, and a headset and the tutor's ability to use the whiteboard during the session. For each of the systems listed in the previous chapter, you can study how to use it before your first class.

The Day of the Class:

First, test your headphone and microphone and enter the online arena before the class time starts.

You might want to post items on the "white board" as if it were an actual white board in a regular classroom. Upload the lesson material by cutting and pasting from your computer.

Focusing on the day's lesson, make a list of what you will cover in the upper right hand corner entitled, Today's Lesson. This will serve as a clear note for students as they get online and start listening and watching the video. (Some may arrive "late" and this will help them see what the lesson is about. In addition, some may not hear you state verbally what the lesson plan is for the day.)

Second, as the students enter the online classroom, welcome them by name (or screen name). This way you can test the microphones and audio right away. (If one of them is having technical problems they can message you and the problem can be eliminated. On the other hand, if students cannot hear your voice because of audio problems, they can message you and tell you right away.)

Third, outline the lesson of the day or Today's Lesson. For example, you can say, "Today we will cover_____(topic).   I   will   talk about_____(subject). If you have a question, wait until I cover this first segment (5-8 minutes, approximately), then ask your questions. Please read what I have written on the board."

Fourth, carry on the lesson by lecturing and writing on the whiteboard. Then engage the student(s) by asking them to reply to your question by 1) speaking into the microphone or by 2) writing on the white board.

 Make sure to give each student time to make an individual response during the class time.

Fifth, before the class time ends, approximately 10 minutes, announce it verbally and on the white board. Leave the last 10 minutes for asking questions and announcing   homework,   with   any   needed explanations.

Each time you teach, use the same pattern.

This is my pattern: I list the day's agenda for the lesson on the top right corner of the white board. Welcome the students. Start the lesson by stating what I will cover in the lesson for that day. Give each student a chance to participate. Save time at the end for questions. Give homework assignments with an explanation.

,You can use your own pattern, of course, but keep it the same each time. I have taught for many years, and one thing I have learned is that simplicity, structure and repetition work best for everyone.

Students will feel comfortable when you provide a structured and predictable setting for learning. When students are comfortable, they can easily learn.

After you learn how to seamlessly use these tools, you can easily manage several students at one time for a small online classroom. Start with one student and then go to two students, then increase to six for an online classroom. You need to manage the students, that is, their responses and questions.

Below is a screenshot of a Virtual Classroom. (Continue reading for a detailed outline of the features of a room.)

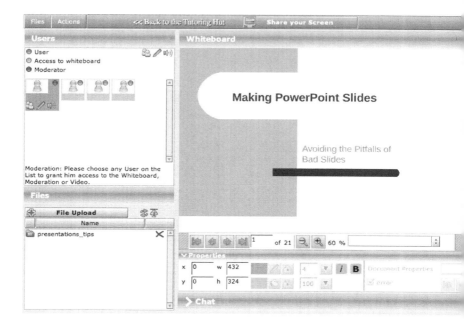

The following numbers correspond to those in the image above:

1) Users Panel:The users panel is the top left box.

•The teacher can see all of the users who are currently in the room

•The teacher can control the users who are permitted to access the whiteboard tools or the webcam

•The users request access to the whiteboard tools and the webcam

2) Files Panel:The files panel is in the lower left box.

•Here you can: upload images, such as Word documents, Powerpoint presentations, PDF files, and others

•You can click to upload a particular page, or an entire presentation directly onto the whiteboard

•You can download uploaded files from the panel to your computer

3) Whiteboard:This is the largest box above where you post your lesson.

4) Whiteboard Tools:

There are numerous whiteboard tools that allow you to write on the board as well as highlight on the board. Students can all read the files that you upload to the whiteboard. This is referred to as the import function which allows you to add text, images or powerpoint files onto the whiteboard. There is a pointer (a black arrow with a red circle around it) where you can point to areas while your students are reading along. You can insert text and highlight it as well as color it. You can save and export your files so that each one of your students can get copies of your lesson.

5) Properties Panel:

•On this section of the panel, you can edit anything created on the whiteboard – text, shapes, lines, arrows, etc.

•You can change colors, height, width and more

6) Webcam Option:

•The teacher controls which user(s) have webcam access

•The teacher controls the size, and location of the webcam screen

•The teacher can choose to use video & audio, or each one individually

•The green circle lights up on the bottom left of the webcam box when you speak

7) At the very bottom of the screen is the chat area where students can type comments or questions to you and to each other. If a student asks a good question, you can type it on the whiteboard for everyone to see. Then you can answer that question. It is comparable to a classroom situation where a student raises their hand to ask a question and the teacher writes the question on the board. This is a good way to emphasize important points.

Chapter 9

The Free Introductory Offer (First Tutoring Session)

The introductory free 1 hour tutoring session will be critical to your success. This way the parents feel they are getting a great deal which they are: a free session with you. Of course they will be impressed with you and their child will continue in the lessons.

Never try and sell a monthly tutoring package without offering the parent a free introductory one hour tutoring session.

Once you provide a good tutoring session, parents will be asking you about your monthly tutoring programs.

If your student's tutoring session goes well and you communicate effectively with the parent, you'll be able to arrange a monthly account.

The key to your introductory offer is to include free bonuses plus a productive one-hour tutoring session. Your initial phone consultation counts as part of the bonus.

If you want to convert a higher percentage of introductory clients, you must sit down and put your bonus together. Just create a valuable bonus for the parent or student.

Here are some ideas:

Motivational tips (for parents)

Study guide (for students)

How to study for tests (for students)

You can find free guides online on these subjects. Just print them out, with their references, and hand them out to parents.

You can make your own guide, in a kind of three folded brochure, and hand them out to every parent. You can use them as advertising and put them in coffee shops and the libraries. Make sure you put your name and email address at the bottom so they can contact you.

Chapter 10

A Website For Your Tutoring Business

I recommend you create a simple website.

Parents will become your client with or without a website. Your knowledge and kindness as a tutor is all you need to impress parents and students.

However, if you want to appear more professional, you can have a website, but don't put a lot of time into it.

Three simple places for a website are as follows: www.wordpress.com, www.blogspot.com , www.yola.com and www.webs.com.

All three of these free blog sites allow you to create a blog that can be formatted to look like a very nice website. Make sure when you set it up to come up with a tutor sounding name for it, like Kim's Tutoring, Craig the Math Tutor or Bay Area Tutor or something that describes yourself, your specialty or your location.

On your website, be sure to include your name, phone number, email address and the subjects you tutor.

You'll also want to give parents a reason to call you. Offer a free demonstration at their home plus a free phone consultation without any obligation.

I recommend including an online photo, which shows parents what you look like so they can trust you.

If you choose to build a more detailed website with a payment system you can do it yourself with a beautiful graphic template like I used from Allwebco Design, www.allwebcodesign.com. I used Allwebco to make my business website http://www.englishwritinghelp.com

The template has several large, colorful graphics that change with each page; and it has animation and a paypal checkout. There are many companies out there that sell website templates, but Allwebco is the best. They are the only website template provider that is very easy to set up and reasonably priced. They have wonderful support.

On the other hand, you can hire someone to help you, like a college student in computer design who may not charge too much.

Chapter 11

Preparing Yourself to Speak With Parents

Step 1: Ask questions about the child's academic situation and whatever difficulties they are experiencing.

Step 2: Give a demonstration of a tutoring session. For example, ask the child questions like what they are having trouble with in school. Then offer solutions. Take a look at their school textbook and attempt to address a problem they are currently having trouble with. Then give them encouragement and end the session with a homework assignment. Offer to set up a second appointment or the first paid tutoring session.

Step 3: Get a yes or no answer whether they will be using you as a tutor. If yes, accept the parent's check and billing address information. I have a student information sheet the parents fill out that includes their address and phone number and their description of their child's problem. They can include information about the times and dates to meet.

Step 4: Thank the parent and assure them that your child will improve with you as their tutor.

By using each of the four steps, you'll be able to introduce your tutoring service to many parents.

Chapter 12

Preparing for Your New Student's First One Hour Introductory Tutoring Session

Before you get started with your first tutoring session, you must do some preparation.

Talk with the student or parent on the phone first. This way, you can find out a few essentials: what subject they need tutoring in, what grade they are in.

Go to the library and get a school book on that area so you can refresh your memory of the subject. On the other hand, you can go online and get information for that student's subject and grade.

Some students may be shy at first, so you may need to do most of the talking to keep things flowing. Asking open-ended questions of the student may help them to open up and feel more comfortable with you. Do you like school? What classes do you have?

Spend some time trying to determine exactly what the student is learning and how their teachers are explaining the content. Ask them to show you their textbook.

Open up the textbook and ask them to show you the chapter they are studying in class.

Be positive and encouraging throughout the session.

Rapport building is important when building trust and a comfortable atmosphere, so make sure you really try to get to know the student beyond just academics. You might want to ask him or her what subjects they like or their hobbies.

Your student's satisfaction is very important if you want to have repeat monthly clients. Your goal is to get them feeling positive so they want to come to the lessons.

Before the conclusion of the session, help the student establish a few short term goals and one-long term goal.

Chapter 13

Guarantee Future Tutoring Sessions with Your Student by Involving Them in the Learning!

Students need to be involved in the learning process to stay interested.

How do you do this?

Set the learning goals with the student, which requires getting them to agree on the goals you are going to help them set. (When times get bad and their motivation is waning, you can refer to this contract to remind them of what they want to accomplish.)

During the first session you will be interacting with the parent, mostly, to set goals for learning. You must also demonstrate to the parent that you can interact with their child in a positive manner, encouraging them but staying in control and making them accountable for the learning goals.

Involving Children in Learning Goals

For example, you can say to them:

"You want to do better in school, Brian, don't you?"

Brian says "Yes."

Then you say, "I am going to help you learn to study better so you can do better in school."

Brian nods in agreement.

"You have to pay attention to me and follow along. I'm going to give a problem to do right now and I need you to do that here at your desk."

"Can you do that for me, Brian?"

Each time the student performs well, give him or her encouragement.

When they balk about doing the work, encourage them.

You can say, "Brian, I am asking you to do this because I know you can do it. I know you are a smart boy; and you can do this work."

Or you can say,"I know this is difficult. Let me help you. We can do it together first."

After saying this, you can then help him do the problem or read a passage and answer a few questions.

Then you can say,

"Now you can try and do it yourself. I will be sitting here."

Then give him or her the math problem or learning task.

After she performs it, say "I knew you could do it!" and smile at him or her.

She will be feeling good about herself.

If the student cannot do the problem or task alone, take them through it again, step-by-step.

Then ask them to do it by themselves while you sit there watching.

If you see him make a mistake, you can say, "Are you sure that is the best choice?" or "Can you think of a better answer or a better solution?"

When you walk the student through a learning task with encouraging words-- while showing your belief in them as a student-- they will come to see themselves this way too.

Eventually they will internalize these study skills and start to believe in themselves.

Children need concrete rewards when they are young.

You can reward them by putting stickers on their work.

Once you start tutoring a student and develop a relationship with him or her, you have the power to do a great thing-- that all teachers aim for-- getting their students curious about learning.

Learning Goals with the Adult Student

Adult students need to be heard. When you are interacting with an adult student you need to satisfy what they perceive as their needs. You need to do this during the first tutoring session. That means you will be asking them questions; and they will be explaining to you their problems. Your chief role at the beginning is to be a listener.

The First Session

When I work with adults, I ask them to tell me what they need or what they are having difficulty with; then we work out a tutoring plan of action. This plan of action is what I will cover with them in the future sessions. During the first session I ask them to fill out a student informational sheet. After they finish I go over it and, at this time, I interview them about their problems and how they would like to improve.

The Interview Questions

The interview questions are aimed at establishing goals for the future, and depend on each individual student's unique situation in life and their plans for the future.

Example 1 Donaldo is a new immigrant. He moved here from Italy. His brother is a citizen here and helped Donaldo secure a job at an automotive repair shop that specializes in paint detailing. Donaldo is excellent at his job because he did detailing for 10 years in Italy. Donaldo cannot communicate with customers well, so he needs to improve his conversational ability in English. (He studied English grammar on his own but his English speaking skills are limited.) In addition, he wants to take the citizenship test in the future.

Tutor: "Donaldo, why do you want to improve your English skills?"

Donaldo: "Speaking the way to make my dreams. I come to America."

Tutor: "Yes. I understand that you came here to America to improve your life."

Donaldo nods his head yes.

Tutor: "Do you use English at your job?"

Donaldo: "I speak only small English." Then Donaldo shakes his head from side to side.

His brother speaks for him. "Donaldo is a smart man. He knows he can't speak English. He wants to be able to make conversations on the job."

Tutor: "Yes, I understand."

Then the tutor writes down the goals for Donaldo and his brother to read. Everything should be written down with a student who has limited English ability, so they can read over it when they go home. Then Donaldo's brother schedules future tutoring sessions.

Example 2

Jessica is a 12 year old in middle school. She's having trouble in Algebra. This is the first time she has taken Algebra. She has never been strong in math, so it is very difficult for her. Her mother tells you that Jessica does very well in language arts. She enjoys reading and writing. She is taking ballet lessons twice a week. Jessica isn't interested in math. She avoids doing the homework because she doesn't know where to start. However, she has to pass the math class to get a good overall average grade so she can go to dance school in the future. Jessica's mother is worried about Jessica's math grade and her poor attitude about doing her homework.

Tutor: "Jessica, I understand that you like ballet."

Jessica: "I love ballet!" she says enthusiastically.

Tutor: "I do too!"

Tutor: "Do you practice ballet?"

Jessica: "Yes!" she laughs."Everyday!"

Tutor: "So how many hours each week do you practice dancing?"

Jessica's mother laughs. Jessica laughs.

Jessica: "20"

Tutor: "That's why you are so good! If you practiced math, you could be good at that too."

Jessica looks bored.

Tutor: "I know you don't like math. Your mother told me. But if you just practice a few hours a week, you will improve. That's all. Just a few hours."

Jessica: "yeah."

Tutor: "I will help you. I can teach you how to do the algebra equation step-by-step. Each time we meet we will take it one step at a time. It's easy. You'll see."

Jessica: "Okay" she says with a smile.

Her mother is smiling and signs Jessica up for future tutoring sessions.

Chapter 14

Building Regular Monthly Income by Getting to Know Your Students and Providing Feedback

All you really have to do is get to know your students as individuals.

But that's simple because you will be seeing them once or more times each week.

Depending upon the student's needs and the money they can spend, you will be seeing them many times in a month.

Take notes on how they are improving, and put it in a student file along with the student information sheet. I find it is easiest to jot down the notes immediately after they leave the tutoring session while it is fresh in my mind.

I keep notes in three main areas: how they did on the homework or assignment(s) I gave them, the tests or homework they completed at school and their attitude. In addition, any information I may get from outside sources such as the parent, a school counselor or a teacher are included here. (Sometimes, but not usually, I have special permission from the parent(s) to talk to the school counselor or their teacher about their progress. In this case, I charge extra for any school meetings.)

Communication is critical to ensure your success as a tutor. Be sure to check in with the parent each month and keep them updated on how their child is doing.

You'll want to discuss the progress that you and your student are making. Ask for feedback from the parents.

Do they see an improvement?

What kind of feedback have they received from the teachers?

Talk about each tutoring session…and more.

You also want to discuss the number of times you are tutoring their child each week. Suggest more or less tutoring sessions, depending on your student's progress. Your parent clients will appreciate this honesty.

Provide the parents with some ideas of what they can do to help you in your tutoring efforts. Parents want to know exactly what they can do to help and reinforce their child's confidence and good grades.

Chapter 15

How to Build Your Tutoring Business without Spending Money

You must either pay money or time to advertise your tutoring service.

In this section, you'll learn how to build your business WITHOUT spending a lot of money.

Technique 1 – Invest in business cards.

When designing your business card, you must decide what you want to offer.

To receive 250 free business cards, go www.vistaprint.com.

You'll have to pay for shipping, but it's still a bargain.

Your business card must include your name, phone number, your email address and your introductory offer.

Put your cards in these locations:

Grocery stores

Libraries

Bookstores

Any place with a community bulletin board

Technique 2 -- Letting parents know about your tutoring service. You can attract students with a brochure or flyer. First, create and have your brochures or flyers printed on professional paper. The more professional this looks, the more calls you'll receive.

Tape the flyers on the doors of the neighborhoods.

You might catch some parents at home if you do this in the afternoon. You can introduce yourself and tell them about your tutoring service.

Technique #3 -- Inform teachers about your tutoring business.

If you can leave business cards in schoolteacher's mailboxes, they can and probably will consider recommending your services to parents. You can go to the school and ask the school's secretary to put your cards inside each teacher's mailbox.

Technique 4 -- If You Ask For Referrals, They Will Come!

There are many ways to go about this. If you choose, you can simply ask for names and numbers of friends from your current clients. Call the parent and let them know who referred you.

Technique5—Sign up with free referral agencies where you can post your services.

Free Tutoring Referral Agencies

http://www.tutormatch.com

Find A Tutor. Very simple to use, free, no sign-up/login, serving USA, UK, Canada, Australia, New Zealand.

tutorprofiles.com. Very easy to use, jus[
postal code and/or city and see a list of l[

Craigslist search under your state and cit)
"Services" and "Lessons".

Local.yahoo.com enter your zip code or cit) ⌐..⊔ state
and then search for tutor.

www.directoryoftutors.com Just type in your zip code
and school level (grade) of the student. Pretty simple!

www.nationaldirectoryoftutors.com. Just enter the
required info and subject matter.

www.orbitutors.com. I found this site to be a bit
complicated and difficult to contact tutors.

www.tutoringservices.com. Not bad, but you have to
sign up and log in, but it's free.

www.findatutor.ca. It's good, but for Canada tutors
only.

There are many others, but you either have to pay, or
the tutors have to pay to be on the list and I'm not too
wild about those companies.

http://www.tutor-ads.com

http://www.tutorvista.com

Chapter 16

How to Build Your Tutoring Business Using Paid Advertising

The ads you create will determine your success, assuming you are targeting the right group of people. It's extremely important for you to measure your cost of advertising vs your return on investment.

Whether you are looking to create copy for newspaper or any other print media, your success depends on three things:

Good ad copy

Targeting the right market

Repetition or frequency of advertising within that market

Ad copy:

The single most important thing in an advertising campaign is good ad copy.

Since we are often asked for newspaper advertising advice, we have come up with a few basic rules to help you create effective newspaper ads.

Each ad you write needs three basic parts:

1.Headline - one or two sentences designed to gain the interest of parents.

2. Body - the meat and potatoes of your offer. Ex. free demo, consultations and assessment.

3.Call to action – encourage the potential client to call for more information.

Different Paid Advertising Methods

1. Newspapers

2. Local publications

3. Magazines

4. School Bus Advertising

5. Billboard advertising

6. Pay-per-click online advertising *must have website

Part Two:

Teaching English to Speakers of Other Languages

Chapter 17

What is an ESL Student?

Getting to Know the ESL Student

As the tutor you need to become acquainted with your student, that means, their life. Knowing something about their everyday life and where they came from will help you determine their needs and how to help them learn English.

This requires asking the right questions and listening, not only to their words but to the emotional content underlying their words.

How do they feel about living in the U.S.?

Even if they do not tell you, you can see that they are nervous or scared by their actions and body language. You can help them feel more confident about their language skills and more relaxed living in the U.S. over the course of tutoring them.

Look at the lists in the next section. These lists will guide you in getting to know your student and where they are in the continuum of experience living in the U.S.

The questions you ask should pinpoint their life experience in this country and their home. Below are sample questions to ask.

•Employment in the U.S. or their home country?

•Education level in their home country?

•Skills used on the job in this country or in their home country?

•How many hours work per week?

•Future employment goals?

•Skills transferable from their home country?

Travel:

Do they have use of other languages?

Do they have knowledge of other cultures?

The possible situations of these students are as follows:

Student at a local university

Work at a shop in this country performing manual labor

Live with a roommate in this country

Live alone in this country and send money back to their family

Unemployed in this country applying for citizenship

Working as a full time employee in this country

Possible situations of these students are as follows:

Wen Shan is a businessman who travels often to China and Hong Kong.

Mr. Kum is a world traveler who speaks several languages and travels to various countries every year. He is now in the U.S. and wants to improve his English.

Some other Questions to Ask to Get to Know Your Student

Is your student new to this country?

When did he arrive?

Did he or she arrive one week ago? One month ago?

Is his or her family in this country now? Are his family members back in his home country?

Why is she living in the U.S. now?

Is she a student?

Is she a new immigrant?

Is he working for an American company?

Is he on a tourist visa?

Is he married to an American?

When you know the answers to these questions, you will know how to help your student. For example, if he is a student at a local university, you know that he must be fairly intelligent and must have passed a rigorous TOFEL exam in order to be accepted into an American university.

If she came here working for a U.S. company and will only be here for 6 months on a limited stay, then you know your goals for helping her learn English will be intensive but short term.

If your student is a new immigrant then you know that he or she will be required to take the citizenship exam and will need to study speaking and listening as well as reading and writing to pass that exam. In addition, you will know that their English language goals are long term. They will need tutoring over a long period of time.

Profiles of ESL Students

There are many kinds of ESL students. Here are some typical profiles:

Michael

Michael is a Korean high school student. (Michael is not his Korean name. He changed it when he moved here from Korea.) He has been living here with his mother for three years. He can speak English but not at a level he is comfortable with. He wants to know English slang. He wants to interact with other American students his own age. He wants to improve his grades. He knows that if he learns more words, he can do better in school. His mother wants him to go to an American university. He needs a tutor so he can get into a good American university.

Jose

Jose is a strawberry picker in a Northern California town. He has three children who are not in school. They help him pick strawberries. His wife sells strawberries at a road side stand. He is very poor since his father snuck into the U.S. illegally; and he never had the chance to get an education. He wants to improve his English so he can get a better job. He wants his children to go to school and have a better life. He needs to learn English so he can get a higher paying job. He wants a job driving truck. He cannot read and cannot fill out a job application. He needs to learn enough English to fill out a job application and to communicate on the job.

Mariko

Mariko is from Japan. She just moved here from Tokyo. She is 24 years old and attends the University of Hawaii. She is very smart and knows English grammar well. Her speaking is very poor. Nobody seems to understand her in her university classes. Her homework is excellent and her papers are written very well. However, she cannot participate in class so her grades are getting lower. She is worried. She needs to improve her English conversation ability. Mariko needs to improve her conversational English.

Chapter 18

The First Meeting with the ESL Student

The first meeting will involve you getting to know the student and them getting to know you.

Student Information Sheet

You should give the student a "Student Information Sheet" that they fill out with their contact information and what they want to learn during their lessons. If they come to the lesson with an English speaking friend, they can help the student communicate with you, if their English level is limited.

Tutor Information Sheet

In addition you can present to them the tutor information sheet about yourself. It should state your name, address and contact information and your fees and time schedule. Any information, such as, special knowledge you have can be included on your information sheet. In addition, you can specify how you tutor.

Suggestions for your first lesson

1. Ask questions and tell about yourself, as in a conversation. Speak slowly. Even if the student doesn't speak very often, remain calm. If they do not speak, ask them to write their words down. Ask them to try again, to say it in English. Once you know what the student can understand you can build on that. For example, if the student says, "My name is Kim." Then you can say, "My name is _____" Then point to

yourself when you say your name. If you ask, "Where are you from?" and the student doesn't reply or seems not to understand, then ask it in a different way. You can say, "I am from America." "Where are you from?" Or you can say, "Your country?" Then wait for an answer.

2. When the student's level is very low it is best if they have a friend come with them for a few tutoring sessions until you are able to communicate with them alone. This will ease the stress level for both of you. It can be quite challenging to teach English through pictures alone; but what I have observed in my many (25 years) of teaching ESL is that these low functioning English speakers learn the most quickly. They suffer very greatly from not having the most basic English skills therefore they are motivated by their inability to function in their everyday life and the humiliation of not having language skills.

Suggested Level 1 Questions for your first Meeting

How are you?

What's your name?

What's your last name?

Please spell your name.

How old are you?

Where are you from?

Did you work in_____?

What did you do there?

Do you have any children?

How many children do you have?

How old are they?

Where do you live now?

Suggested Level 1 Questions using objects

Lay coins out on the table or desk. Say, "Show me a nickel."

Where is 25 cents?

Please give me 42 cents.

How much is this? (Give the student 44 cents)

Give me a quarter.

What is this? (Show the student a check)

What is a check used for?

Take out your watch or a clock and set it on the table or desk.

What time is it?

Show me 8:30 on the clock.

What time do you get up in the morning?

Show me on the clock what time you get up.

Take a calendar and put it on the table or desk in front of you.

When is your birthday?

Show me your birthday on the calendar.

Show me Friday, Monday, March, July…

Show me the number 5, 21, 17, 30 etc.

Take out a note pad and write the alphabet on it.

Show me the letter f,g,h,k,l etc.

Open the note pad to a blank page and ask the student to write down numbers and letters. Ask them verbally to do the following.

Write the number 7, 85, 43, 3, 12…

Write the letter b, n ,m ,u ,l etc.

In addition, use objects in the room and ask the student what it is. For example, hold a small pencil sharpener in your hand and ask, "What is this?" Point to the door knob and ask, "What is this?

Student Information Sheet

Name:_____

_____

Address:_ ·_____

_____

Phone:_____Email:_____

_____

What do you want to improve in your use of English?

Reading   Speaking   Writing   Listening

Pronunciation

(Please circle)

How   long   will   you   be   here   in   this
country?_____

How   often   do   you   want   to   have
lessons?_____

_____

_____

What   languages   do   you
speak?_____

What   languages   do   your   parents
speak?_____

Tutor Information Sheet

Your name

Address

Phone/Email

Website

Fees

Teaching/Tutoring Style: State whether you will tutor one-on-one or in small groups or online.

(See pages 19-22 for similar information in the Contact Sheet)

Location: State whether you will tutor in the student's home or a neutral location, like a library or coffee shop.

Chapter 19

Tips for Speaking with ESL Students

1. Communication is the goal, so do not focus on language. Instead, focus on what is being said. Have an activity planned that has an interesting topic then work with the student to use language to discuss that topic.

2. All activities that help communication are good. Pictures, games, field trips, excursions.

3. Focus on communicating, not on errors.

4. Don't fill up the silence. Wait and let the student speak when he or she is ready.

5. Don't raise your voice when you have to repeat something. Just be patient and repeat it again.

6. Rephrase a question or statement when the student doesn't understand it the first time.

7. Say, "Do you understand?" to make sure they understand.

8. Get to know the students interests and focus on that as a topic.

9. Go from simple to complex. If the student can answer a yes or no question, then do that for a while. Later, you can move on to a more difficult question like comparing two things.

Using a menu with photos as a way to teach English

If you take a menu from a family restaurant like Denny's, you can make copies of it and use it to teach English.

First you can open the menu and ask a question that only requires a yes or no answer.

For example, point to the dish with a hamburger and ask, "Do you like hamburgers?"

The student answers, "yes."

Next, ask a question that requires them to use more words to make an answer.

You can point to the dish with the hamburger and ask, "What kind of meat is this?" You can ask, "Is this bread or a bun?" when pointing to the hamburger bun.

You can point to the french fries beside the hamburger and ask, "What are these?"

You can ask "How much does the hamburger and French fries cost?"

You can ask the student to role play with you where you are the waitress and they are the customer. They have to order a dish for their lunch.

The most important thing to remember is: communication is the goal not perfection. As ESL Instructors we seek fluency in our students, not grammatically perfect sentences. Therefore we teach language as it is spoken in conversation. We can use idioms and/or slang too.

Free Talking: "FRIENDS"

1) What can you see in the foreground of the picture? (사진의 전경)
2) What can you see in the background of the picture? (사진의 배경)
3) Where do you think this is?
4) Who do you think these people are?
5) What are they doing?
6) What are they wearing?
7) What are they holding?
8) How old are they?
9) What time of day do you think it is?
10) Why are they here?
11) What are they saying?

Pairs or Groups

1. Look at the picture.
2. Answer the questions.
3. Free talking!

12) Do you have any male friends?
13) Do you have any female friends?
14) Do you have a boy/girl-friend?
15) Do you have a special friend?
16) Do you like having friends?
17) Do you like talking to friends?
18) Do you spend much time with friends?
19) Do you tell your friends everything?
20) What is a "Good friend"?
21) **Free-talking** Friends

A friend
in need
is
a friend
indeed!

- 15 -

You can use the above photo and questions to encourage conversation and guide their use of

97

English. For example, I would first ask the easiest questions:

1. Is there a man in the picture? Is there a woman in the picture?

Then I would proceed to more difficult questions where they have to use more words to answer.

2. What are the man and woman doing? If the student cannot answer, you can say, "They are eating." Or "They are on a picnic." Or "They are sitting on a blanket."

After these most basic questions, ask questions 1 to 11 on the handout above. If the student can answer these easily proceed to questions 12 through 21. The questions 12 through 21 are much more difficult because they require the student to compose sentences on their own, about themselves.

Note: If the student has difficulty answering questions 1 through 11 then do not ask the harder questions. Just teach them the correct answers to questions 1 through 11.

You can repeat this process with many different situations, in order to teach them vocabulary and conversation skills. What I do is clip pictures from old magazines. Then I use those pictures as a springboard for teaching conversation. (See Chapters 22 and 24)

Chapter 20

The Lesson Plan

Each lesson should be planned according to a simple goal and be able to be achieved in 50 minutes to one hour.

Objective for
Lesson:_____

1. Review from prior lesson

2. Review materials for today's lesson objective

3. Introduce new vocabulary

4. Introduce conversation activity using the vocabulary

5. Practice the conversation

6. Pronunciation

Sample Lesson Plan

Objective: Student will be able to call on the phone and ask about apartments for rent.

1. Review what student learned at the previous lesson

2. Review vocabulary for today's lesson: apartment, 2BR apt., two bathroom, rental, condominium, duplex, utilities, ad in newspaper, do you take pets, security deposit

3. Introduce activity: what dialogue to use on the phone to ask for information

Hello. My name is _____. I saw your ad in the newspaper for a 2 bedroom apartment. Can you tell me more about it? Has it been rented? Are pets allowed? Is it located in a secure building? Is a security deposit required? Can I look at it? Can I bring a friend? When is it available? Is there a lease? Is there a parking lot?

4. Practice the dialogue with the student. Go back and forth between yourself and the student, as if you are the landlord.

5. Practice using role play

6. Pronunciation practice based upon the student's weaknesses. For example, whenever I notice that a student mispronounces a word, I make a note of it so I can later teach them how to pronounce correctly.

Chapter 21

Assessing the Students Level of English Usage

First of all, a tutor needs to know where the student is at now, in terms of their English speaking ability, before he or she can help them progress to the next level.

The lowest level student is one who cannot use English to communicate in everyday life. If the student cannot communicate with you well at the first meeting then they do not possess the basic survival skills to function using English in everyday life.

Your goal as a tutor is to help them progress through the survival skills and beyond. After students progress in their English use through the survival skills they can go even further and learn to study in English. For example, they can read newspapers and discuss news topics.

As you look over the levels of survival skills you need to determine what your student can do. If your student cannot even perform at level one, in using English, then you must teach them level one survival skills. If your student can do level one but not level two then you can teach them level two skills.

Level One (English speaking) Survival Skills

1. The student can express their lack of understanding.

2. The student understands the concept of same and different, left to right and top down sequencing.

3. The student can identify letters and print letters.

4. The student can identify numbers and print numerals.

5. The student can identify U.S. money: coins and bills.

6. The student can do basic addition and subtraction with money.

7. The student can read and write amounts of money.

8. The student can read clock time and digital time.

9. The student can read calendar dates and numerical dates.

10. The student can understand and respond to: "how much?" "What time?" "Where?" and "what?"

11. The student understands family and personal identification.

12. The student can write his or her first and last name.

Level Two Survival Skills

1. The student can sign or endorse a check.

2. The student can buy stamps at the post office.

3. The student can identify basic colors and geometric shapes.

4. The student can identify common household furnishings.

5. The student can identify over-the-counter medicines.

6. The student can ask for help by dialing 9-1-1

7. The student can go to a neighbor's home and ask for help

8. Given a phone number, the student can dial it.

9. The student can identify typical articles of clothing

Level Three Survival Skills

1. The student can buy a money order.

2. The student can show identification when cashing a check or taking out a video.

3. The student can identify the simplest jobs and the responsibilities involved.

4. The student can identify good work skills.

5. The student can identify body parts and common symptoms of injury or illness.

6. The student can call for emergency help and clearly state and spell their name and address.

7. The student can recognize vocabulary related to housing rentals.

8. The student can understand warnings on bottles and containers such as poison, danger etc.

9. The student can identify themselves on the phone and ask for the person with whom she wants to speak.

Level Four Survival Skills

1. The student can fill out a change of address card.

2. The student can go to the bank and fill out deposit and withdrawl slips.

3. The student can fill out a check to pay a bill.

4. The student can understand common employment terms such as full-time, part-time, benefits, sick pay, health insurance etc.

5. The student can ask questions about job duties, hours, wages, pay, overtime etc.

6. The student can call in sick at work.

7. The student can make or change medical appointments or dental appointments

8. The student can describe needed housing repairs and utility problems.

9. The student can fill out person information forms such as movie rental applications or bank account applications or rental application.

Level Five Survival Skills

1. The student can keep a record the amount, date and new balance for their checking account.

2. The student can register children in preschool, day care or school.

3. The student can describe vaccinations and the rules regarding them.

4. The student can describe his or her employment skills, experience, preferences on a job application.

5. The student can call a potential employer and ask about a job.

6. The student can identify several jobs for which they are qualified and describe the duties and responsibilities involved in them.

7. The student can read and respond to common instructions and warning signs at work.

8. The student can read and explain housing wanted ads.

9. The student can name the common body parts and basic internal body functioning.

Level Six Survival Skills

1. The student can fill out Federal and State income tax short forms.

2. The student can explain types of loans and credit card terms.

3. The student can participate in parent-teacher conferences.

4. The student can explain some of the most basic legal responsibilities involved in a driver's license or health insurance

5. The student can ask questions about job performance and job expectations.

6. The student can list the aspects of a successful job interview.

7. The student can read aloud and explain employment wanted ads.

8. The student can fill out a job application.

9. The student can list the personal responsibilities and social behavior necessary to keep a job.

10. The student can explain pay check deductions and check accuracy.

11. The student can explain future employment goals.

12. The student can explain his or her health insurance plan benefits and exclusions.

13. The student can demonstrate comparison shopping.

14. The student can follow a map to a destination.

The source for these Survival Skills Summaries are as follows:Esler, Megan. Portland Community College. June 1982.

Chapter 22

Teaching the Beginner

A student with very limited English usage will need pictures and objects in order to learn basic vocabulary. You can show them a children's picture dictionary or clips of photos from magazines. Point to objects in the dictionary or the photos and teach them the word by speaking it and writing it down.

Ask the student to look at this photo.

Point to an item in the photo and ask, "What is this?"

The student will answer. Teach them to say, "This is a measuring cup." Or "These are measuring spoons." Or "These are measuring scoops." Or "This is flour."

Make Simple Sentences

After you teach them some vocabulary, then you can work at putting simple sentences together with a verb.

This is a measuring cup. The measuring cup is half full. Or The measuring cup is half full of oil.

Subject + Verb +Object.

After introducing many of these simple sentences then you can use more complex sentences with prepositions.

The measuring scoops are sitting in flour.

Subject+Verb+preposition.

The next sentence structures you can introduce are questions.

What is in the measuring cup?

Where are the measuring scoops?

Using Pictures with Simple Vocabulary

When you teach with pictures or photos make everything into a conversation.

Keep it simple by choosing pictures with one object or a group of the same objects. Use objects they already know or see in their everyday life.

What are these?

These are cherries.

What color are the cherries?

The cherries are red and yellow.

How many cherries are there?

There are five cherries.

Do you like cherries?

You can start by using pictures to teach them basic vocabulary with simple sentence structures.

After you teach using pictures or photos with simple objects, you can proceed to scenes. Scenes have multiple objects and show action and emotion.

Ask the student simple questions about the photo.

Is there a man in the photo? What is he doing?

Is there a woman in the photo? What is she doing?

What are they sitting on? What is the color? Are there pillows in the picture?

What are they doing?

What are they eating?

Are they friends? Boyfriend and girlfriend? Husband and wife?

Are they having a good time?

How do you know that? Are they happy? Sad? Angry?

More difficult:

Make up a sentence about the photo and write it down for the student.

The man and woman are sitting on the sofa eating almonds. They are laughing.

Diagram the sentence into two simple parts:

"The man and woman" is the subject.

"Sitting on the sofa eating almonds" is the preposition.

"They" is the subject and "are laughing" is the preposition.

Diagram the sentence in a more detailed way:

"The" is an article which is used to introduce the subject. "man and woman" is the subject.

Sitting is the verb. The verb shows action. "On the sofa" is the preposition. Prepositions show a position. "Eating" is the verb. "Almonds" is the object.

This is the first level for using photos. You can use these simple descriptions for many different photos you can find in a magazine. In addition to using magazine articles, you can use objects.

After you teach with photos that show scenes, you can proceed to photos showing a process.

The process can be as simple as preparing a simple dish.

Cook until just set around the edge. Scramble gently. Turn off the heat as soon as the bottom has set.

Sprinkle the cheese down the middle. Fold one-third of the omelet toward the center. Fold again and flip onto a plate

This progression of photos shows how to make a simple omelet.

The idea is to get the student to describe the process. This is an exercise for more advanced students, after they have already learned the vocabulary and objects for cooking. For example, they already know what a skillet is and what eggs are and what cheese is and the colors black, yellow and red.

You can ask the student:

How can I make a cheese omelet?

They have to describe the process in the photo.

Some typical words they will have to use are: first, second, third, fourth, fifth. Some other words they might use are: step one, step two…

You can get photos from old cooking magazines or women's magazines to show them the photo for them to describe.

Some other typical processes are:

What do you do when you get up in the morning?

How do you drive a car?

How do you use a washing machine?

Teaching Conversation using a Map

Teaching conversation using a map is an old technique that all ESL instructors are familiar with because it is effective; and it is an easy way for them to learn English. You can easily teach them how to listen to and give directions using a map. In addition, you teach them how to use reference points, to give and receive directions.

Waikiki Beach

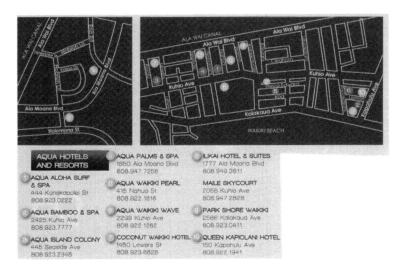

This is a map of Waikiki Beach.

First, show them the map and the key to the hotels on the map that are noted with dots. Ask them to listen to you give directions first. You can start by saying, "I am starting from the Aqua Aloha Surf and Spa and then I am going to the Ilikai Hotel." Then give them step by step directions, using phrases like "turn right at --- street" and "turn left at ---street", "on the left hand side" or "on the right hand side." You can also use phrases like "across the street from" and "at the corner of."

Ask them to point on the map where you start and your path to the end location.

After the student is comfortable following your directions, ask them to give directions to you. Make sure they give detailed directions such as start at this hotel then turn left at a certain street and turn right at a specific street then on the right side is the certain hotel.

This is a difficult task for most ESL students. However it is critical for them to learn. They need to be able to do this in everyday life. (I lived in Japan for six years and I had to learn to receive and give directions in Japanese. I frequently got lost in Japan whether in my car or walking on the sidewalk. When someone is new to a culture they often get lost because there are so many cues that they simply do not understand. This is why learning to understand and give directions are so critical to everyday life.)

Using Objects to Teach ESL: I often used a box of objects to help my students learn new words. (Objects are a stimulus to building vocabulary.) For female students, it is especially useful to bring in a box of kitchen utensils.

Bring in a box of objects from your kitchen:

Spatula

Fork

Spoon

Coffee cup

Glass

Ask the student the name of the item.

For example, if you set a fork in front of them, the correct answer is "fork". Then you can teach them to use it in a sentence. For example, "This is a fork." Then move the fork away from them. Ask them to point to it and say, "That is a fork." Do the same exercise with many objects. Through this simple exercise they will learn to identify objects that are near and far away, using "this" and "that".

Then you can teach them to make different sentences with the same objects. For example, "I eat with a fork." "She eats with a fork." Or "He eats with a fork." Or "He does not have a fork." "She has a fork." "I use a fork to eat." "She uses a fork to eat." "He uses a fork to eat." "We use a fork to eat." Through this simple exercise, you can show them how to use pronouns, such as, she, he, they and we.

You can teach them how to use more complicated speech with the same object.

For example, "In the U.S., we use a fork to eat." "In Japan, we use chopsticks to eat."

"Today I will use a fork to eat." "Tonight I will use chopsticks to eat."

When you introduce a new sentence form, reinforce it with repetition. Use multiple objects in the same sentence form, so they can understand it through repeating it over and over again. Let them use their translator to look up the words in their own language.

Teaching the ESL student basic vocabulary is similar to what a preverbal child learns. However, unlike a child, they already possess a large conceptual vocabulary (in their own language) for most of the objects and concepts. Because of this, the electronic bilingual dictionary is a useful tool as well as a translator.

Homework

After the teaching part of the lesson is over, give them homework.

Give them a list of 10 simple words that refer to concrete objects, like bear, cup, sofa etc.

Ask them to look these words up in their bilingual dictionary or translator at home. (The next lesson you teach them sentences with these new words.)

Types of Vocabulary

Concrete

Stick to teaching the beginner concrete vocabulary words. What concrete vocabulary means is: when you show them a picture of a cat they know what it is and can easily name it in their own language.

This indicates they understand the concept but not the correct word in English. Therefore, unlike a child, you are not introducing concepts when you teach simple vocabulary, you are just teaching names. For example, a Japanese person will say "neiko" when you show them the picture of a cat.

You can find the title of a picture dictionary on an internet bookstore. Ask them to buy it and work with that book to develop vocabulary quickly. In addition, you can bring magazines to the tutoring session and work with the pictures in the magazine. Only introduce a limited number of new vocabulary each lesson. Every few lessons review the vocabulary you taught them in the past. (You want them to remember the vocabulary.)

Each student has a maximum learning point and you can get to know that as you work with each student. Some students can learn 4 or 5 new words each lesson but other students may only be able to learn 3. Some students can memorize easily but when it comes to making a conversation using the new vocabulary, it is more difficult. In most cases, after 3 or 4 lessons you can understand their learning point. Sometimes it takes a little longer.

Organizing the Lesson

What I have discovered after many years of tutoring is that establishing a organized tutoring format makes it easier for the student to learn and easier for me to teach the lesson. For example, as soon as I sit down with the student, I ask, "How are you today?" The student will respond. Then I will ask them for their homework and go over the homework assignment. Then I will introduce the day's lesson. Then I will ask them if there is something that they do not understand. I will then listen to them and answer any questions they have. Finally, I will give them homework. Creating a lesson pattern for the student will make them feel more relaxed because they will soon discover what is expected of them. When they are more relaxed, they can learn better.

Abstract Vocabulary

Abstract vocabulary refers to ideas, concepts, feelings and more academic words.

Some examples of these words are as follows:

Fantastic

Sad

Vague

Happy

Democracy

Moody

Relative

Stranger

Administration

When teaching these words it is useful to group them together. For example, words we use to talk about the government, or words we use to describe our family, or words we use to express emotions.

The tutor needs to work with the student to "use" the vocabulary in a conversation. This is where most of the tutoring work comes into play, teaching them how to "use" English.

After introducing a vocabulary word, you can compose a few sentences that follow each other in a mock conversation style, so the student can practice with you.

There are many ESL conversation books that contain these kinds of simple conversations that you can have the student practice with you during the lesson. Usually there is a CD that the student can listen to, so they can listen and practice speaking at home. Have them bring it to the tutorial and go over it with them so they can listen and understand what is being said.

Idioms

Idioms are another type of language that ESL students need to learn. I suggest using a textbook like *Idioms For Everyday Use,* Milada Broukal or *Essential Idioms in English,* Robert James Dixson. Each chapter is laid out according to one idiom. It has pictures and lessons and sample conversation for the student to follow. Idioms are fun to teach.

Give Action Homework

In addition to the lessons, you can assign them "action" homework, where they have to "use" English in the world, in order to complete the assignment.

For example, ask the student to go to a McDonalds, and go up to the cashier's register, and ask the cashier where the rest room is located. You can give him or her specific instructions about what to say and how to say it. Then assign it for homework. The next lesson, ask them what happened. If they were not successful, ask them what happened. Then work with the student to iron out the problem. Give them the same action homework assignment again. Then ask them what happened the following lesson.

Over time, after the student completes multiple action homework assignments, he or she will realize what problems they are having and how to deal with them.

Action Homework

Sample: Action Homework

Go to McDonald's and order a kids meal with hamburger.

Ask for a special order. Ask for the hamburger to be plain.

Student will report on what happened at the next lesson.

After the student has done the homework, ask them what happened.

Tutor can ask: Did the cashier understand your request?

Did she ask you any other questions? Did you understand her?

Was your hamburger plain?

Did the student go alone or were they with a friend?

Sample: Action Homework

Go to the Library and apply for a Library Card

Ask the Librarian for an application

Fill out the application

Return the Application to the Librarian

Listen to What the Librarian Says

What did she ask you for?

Show her your identification.

What identification did you show her?

Student will report on what happened at the next lesson.

You can ask: What library did you go to?

Did you go alone?

Did the librarian understand your request?

What did she say?

Did you fill out the application?

What did the librarian ask you after you gave her the application?

Did you understand her?

Did you ask her to repeat?

What identification did you show her?

Did you receive the library card?

What happened?

At the next lesson you can ask the student to report to you what happened.

Chapter 23

Teaching the Students at their Level Using Questions

Appropriate Questions at Varying Levels

The types of questions we ask students elicit different kinds of responses that go from easy to difficult. The easiest question requires only a yes or no answer. The more detailed questions require more English ability to answer.

1. Do you like hamburger? (yes or no)

2. Do you like McDonald's hamburgers or Burger King's hamburgers? (Choice: this or that)

3. Where can you get a good hamburger? (Wh-question)

4. What is in a good hamburger?

5. How much does a hamburger cost?

6. Why are hamburgers so popular in the U.S.?(Why-question)

Start students out at the yes or no questions and move toward the more difficult questions that require more language skills to answer.

The key is to keep the student struggling to keep up but don't make the lesson so difficult that they feel like giving up.

If the student is good at answering "this or that" questions, like "I prefer _____ to _____. " or "I like granola but I don't like cheerios." Then keep asking them questions at this level during the conversation but lead them into more difficult "What" "Where" and How" questions that require more language skills to answer. "How are cheerios different from granola?" "Where can you buy cheerios?"

Chapter 24

Teaching ESL Using Pictures

Pictures are the gateway to teaching the ESL student. It doesn't matter where they are from or how well they can speak English, they will recognize pictures.

Pictures contain universal objects and meanings: objects such as a bowl, a cat, a woman, a child or a house are things everyone knows.

Pictures show feelings such as warmth, anger, happiness and love. However, describing feelings require vastly different levels of language ability.

Concrete Objects

Looking at a picture of a cat is simple. It is what it is. Everyone knows what a cat is even if they do not know the English word "C-A-T".

Representational Objects or Pictures that Represent Something

Looking at a woman who is staring out from a train window with tears falling down her face is more difficult to describe.

We can say she is crying. But why is she crying? One student might say she is sad. Another student will say she is missing her husband or child. We could say that she is saying goodbye to a person she is leaving behind or to a city she is leaving.

In addition, it conveys so many subtle meanings that this type of picture can serve as a springboard to discussing feelings and concept such as leaving, saying goodbye moving from one country to another. There are endless possibilities, which is why pictures are a major tool for teaching ESL.

There is a lot the teacher or tutor can learn about the ESL student through pictures which is why we use pictures for assessment or for determining how they are currently able to use English for communication.

Using Pictures for Assessment:

Hold up a picture of a cat. (Cut out from a magazine.)

Ask the student, "what is this?"

Then see how the student responds.

She should respond, "This is a cat." However, she may say, "This is cat." Or "cat." Then you can teach her the correct sentence, "This is a cat."

Hold up a picture of a woman and ask, "What is this?"

Then see how the student responds.

She should respond, "This is a woman." or "This is an old woman." She may say, "This is woman." Or "This woman." Or "woman" You can teach her the correct sentence form. You can also add other descriptions, depending upon the exact picture, like "This is an old woman." Or "This is a woman wearing a winter coat." etc.

Notice: Can the student say only one word, like "cat" or "woman". Or can the student say, "This is a cat." And "This is a woman."

Write it down in your notebook what the student is able to do. I usually only write a few simple notes so I remember what this student is able to do with English. Then before the next lesson I can review it.

Using Pictures for Teaching:

Remember: we only have to use pictures with students who are not able to speak in simple sentences.

Hold up a picture of a cat and say "cat." Tell the student to respond by repeating after you, "cat." After she repeats this, then form a short sentence with this word. Say, "This is a cat." Then ask the student to repeat after you. "This is a cat."

Use this same process with many different pictures. You can also use a children's picture dictionary. You can get one at a local public library.

Show the student this picture and ask, "What are these?"

She may say, "cherries"

She may say, "These are cherries."

She might not know. In this case, you can point to the photo and say, "cherries."

Show the student this picture and ask, "What are these?"

He may say, "nuts" He may say, "These are nuts." Maybe he doesn't know what they are. In this case you can say, "These are hazel nuts."

You can go onto many simple photos to help them learn vocabulary. It is best to choose vocabulary of things in their everyday environment, such as, stove, refrigerator, table, house, cat, etc. After you teach them to name items then you can move on to simple sentences and more complex sentences or questions.

Show the student this photo. Ask them, "What is this?" The correct answer is, "This is a fruit salad." After you teach them the name you can teach them the fruit names. For example, "A fruit salad contains bananas, grapefruit, oranges, pineapple and apples."Then you can point to each item and say, "This is a piece of pineapple." "This is a banana slice." "This is an orange slice."

Hints: About choosing photos it is always best to use items from the student's everyday life so they can apply what they are learning. Get a menu with photos. A menu is very good for the ESL student because they will encounter menus a lot in their daily life.

In addition, take the student outside and point to items. Ask them, "What is that?" to something far away. Then point to something nearer and say, "What is this?" Then sit down and make a few simple sentences about those items. Teach him or her the new vocabulary in simple sentences.

You can make up a simple dialog to follow with the student. Take turns with the parts, part A(asking questions) and part B(answering questions).

Dialog with a Picture

"What are these?"

"These are plums."

"How many plums are there?"

"There are two plums."

"What color are the plums?"

"The plums are red."

"Do you like plums?"

"Yes, I like plums." Or "No, I do not like plums." Or "I have never eaten plums."

"Do you eat plums?"

"No. I don't eat plums."

"Where can you get plums?"

"You can get plums in the grocery store."

"Are plums a fruit or vegetable?"

"Plums are a fruit."

Chapter 25

Teaching Pronunciation

Improving Fluency vs Seeking Perfection

The goal of teaching pronunciation is to help the student improve their skills, not to make them speak perfect English.

Very few international people can speak English with the same pronunciation as a native born speaker of English. But we do not expect them to. What we aim to do as teachers and tutors is to improve their fluency, that is, their ability to use English in everyday life.

The first step is to know what pronunciation difficulties the student is having now. The professional ESL Instructor gives the student an assessment to determine their level of pronunciation. As a tutor there is a similar way you can determine the student's speaking level.

Give the student a handout of a typical conversation. (See "At the Video Store" handout). Keep a copy of the handout in front of you. Ask the student to read each line. As he or she reads each line, you circle the words that are mispronounced.

After they finish reading, ask them to repeat the words they mispronounced again. Write these words down in your notes.

The second step is for you to read the handout slowly to the student and ask them to listen closely to how you pronounce the words. (Have them follow along, looking at the handout, as you read.)

Next, ask the student to read out one sentence, then you read out the same sentence. Do it twice and ask them to listen to the difference.

The first few times, the student will probably not be able to hear the difference between how you pronounce a word and how they pronounce it. After you begin your pronunciation lessons they will gradually be able to hear the difference and then slowly they will improve their own speaking. It takes time. Listening comes first, then hearing and finally speaking.

Ask the student to bring a recording device to class and record your voice on it for them, reading out their mispronounced words, slowly.

Part of their homework will be listening to your recording. In addition, ask them to bring a hand held mirror to class for pronunciation exercises.

The major work in teaching the student to pronounce words correctly is achieved in three parts:

1.) Teaching them to listen well and to notice the difference between words that sounds very similar, except for one sound. The process involves "minimal pairs" exercises.

2.) Helping the student to notice how they are physically positioning their mouth to say a word. I will explain more below. The process involves mirror work.

3.) Modeling for the student how to pronounce a sound and then changing their way of sounding out a word.

Listening Exercises

Using listening exercises, to improve pronunciation, is a way to make the student more aware of how a specific letter sounds. This kind of listening is very detailed and done in very short sequences. You can use a CD or anything you want. The key is allow them to listen to a very short passage, just one sentence or two depending upon how difficult it is for them.

I record my own voice on my handheld audio recorder. I only record a few sentences. I say it very slowly into the recorder. Then I play it during the tutoring session and ask the student what they hear. For example, I use words that I know they have a hard time pronouncing. I play one sentence only then ask the student what they heard. Usually, they get it wrong. Then I play it over again, word by word. I replay it again. In addition, I say the word or words, they do not hear, out loud and then I write them down on paper. Then I play it again. Finally, the student will be able to hear it.

Mirror Work

Mirror work is a technique I use for teaching pronunciation. It involves the student looking into the mirror and noticing where their tongue and teeth are when they make a particular sound. It also requires that they notice the amount of air that they push through their mouth to make the sound.

For example, producing the "t" sound

The sound "t" requires that the speaker's teeth are together and the air in the mouth is pushed forward as the sound is being made. If you look at yourself in the mirror as you pronounce "t" you will notice this.

When working with the student, using mirror work, let them hold the mirror up in front of themselves as they make the sound. After they do it, hold the mirror up in front of yourself and make the same sound. Show the student where your teeth and tongue are inside your mouth to make that particular sound.

You can then ask the student to change the position of their tongue or teeth or the amount of air they push out, to make the correct sound. This method is very intensive and takes time, but is very effective over the long term. I use this method for only about 10 minutes during one tutoring session since it is very detailed and is something they can practice at home after I have helped them pinpoint the correct mouth position.

Minimal Pair Exercises

First choose words that sound alike except for one sound, such as pat, fat, hat and tat. The teacher says the word first, fat. Then the student says the word, fat.

Then the teacher says the word pat, emphasizing the sound of "p". Then the student says the word pat. Then the teacher says the word "fat" emphasizing the sound of "f" and then "pat" emphasizing the sound of "p." Then the student repeats after the teacher. Each time the teacher watches the student's lips as they sound the word and listens to the sound they produce. This exercise is called minimal pairs and can be found in pronunciation textbooks. It is a traditional method and it works. It is quite intensive, takes time and proceeds slowly. However, it is essential because research in the field of linguistics have shown that mispronounced words are the root of all misunderstandings for international people when they are trying to learn English.

Focus on the sound not the spelling.

An excellent book on pronunciation is: PD's: Pronunciation Drills for Learners of English by Edith Crowell Trager and Sarah Cook Henderson. This excellent pronunciation text lists up minimal pair exercises according to specific pronunciation problems.

The best part about this book is it categorizes typical pronunciation problems of people according to their native language and country. For example, typical pronunciation problems of native speakers of Japanese are listed with references to specific pages of the book where there are lessons that are designed for these Japanese students.

At the Video Store: a Pronunciation Handout

Customer: I want to rent movies.

Cashier: Are you a member?

Customer: What is that?

Cashier: A member has a video card. (She shows the student a plastic video membership card.)

Customer: No. I do not have this card.

Cashier: You can fill out this application. (She hands the student a membership card application to fill out.)

Customer: I have a question. How much does it cost?

Cashier: It is free to be a member. To rent a movie costs five dollars each.

Customer: How can I pay?

Cashier: You can use your credit card. Or you can pay cash. But you have to have a credit card on file.

Customer: I don't understand.

Cashier: You must have a credit card or debit card to be a member.

Customer: Can I get a movie today?

Cashier: Yes. After you complete the membership application, you can rent movies today.

Chapter 26

Teaching ESL Listening Skills with Podcasts

What is a podcast? A podcast is a media file that can be used as a learning tool.

You can use podcasts from the Internet. The students can learn to listen to how natural English is used.

Listen to the Podcast Before Using it with Student

When you listen to a podcast before using it with the student, you will notice two things: It is very interesting and it is difficult to understand for international students. But that is the beauty of it. It makes students "stretch" their listening ability. They will have to listen closely and several times before they understand it. However, after several lessons using podcasts, their listening and conversation skills will improve.

There are many listening resources on the internet. A podcast is a media file (.mp3, .wma, .mp4) uploaded to the Internet by an individual, radio station, or any company or organization. Podcasts are usually free and can be downloaded and saved directly to the computer.

Podcasts

The quality of the podcasts are varied, from amateur to professional. The English on some is moderately difficult, while others are very difficult, and are spoken rapidly, with a lot of slang or idioms.

The tutor needs to choose the podcast to fit the Using the podcast in the tutorial

student's level. The interests of a student are also important. If a student is interested in sports, give her a sports podcast where news about sports events or the players are discussed.

A podcast can be downloaded to the student's computer, portable .mp3 player, or portable storage device. After the file is saved, it can be burned to a CD. Students can use this to practice listening comprehension at home (from their computers or CD players) or on the go.

I use podcasts during the tutoring session, with a handout, to make sure that the student focuses on specific words, tenses or grammar structures.

Find out what the student is interested in, then design the podcast lesson around those interests, devoting one lesson to a certain field of interest, then another lesson to a different one.

The tutor can also use news podcasts, focusing on current issues and events.

How to use a podcast in the tutoring session

Using a podcast in the tutorial gives the tutor a great deal of freedom. She may use the podcast only for listening comprehension, or she may use it as a basis for an entire lesson. For this article, let us look at how a podcast can be used for a full lesson.

Choosing the podcast

Finding out what the student is interested in is the tutor's first task. Once interest is determined, a podcast can be chosen. Finding a podcast is easy. One can use an Internet search engine or download free software which searches for podcast media files without going to any web page.

One of the best podcast sites is National Public Radio (NPR). All of the podcasts can be downloaded for free, and they have a quite extensive list of topics, ranging from environmental interest to controversial issues. One podcast may even include a variety of topics, "NPR Shuffle," a daily sampler of popular NPR programs.

Practically speaking, the instructor must decide how she is going to play the podcast for the student. If she has access to a CD or DVD player, then she will have had to have burned a CD before class time.

If she has a laptop, she can play the audio file directly. Laptop speakers are loud enough to be used in the room with one student. Make sure you have a private area for this lesson or a corner in the coffee shop.

Using a Handout

It is a good idea to make a handout to go with the podcast. This makes the lesson structured and focuses the students' attention on what you want them to get out of the lesson. Engage the student. Ask his or her opinion. Make the handout contain different kinds of exercises. Here is a design of a podcast worksheet I designed.

Topic. The topic, taken from an NPR Shuffle podcast, was about meeting people on facebook, through the Internet.

Warm Up. I listened to a few minutes at home, picking out key vocabulary I thought the student probably did not know. I put these words in the first section of the worksheet and gave the student 10 minutes to look these words up in his dictionary. Any words he already knew he could skip. This was a pre-listening exercise.

Warm Up. In this next section, the student read a question related to the podcast theme of socializing via facebook: What do you think is the most important way to get to know a new person on the internet? This is a discussion and writing exercise. The student has 5 minutes to write his answer. This is also a pre-listening exercise.

Content (Listen and Answer). Now it is time to actually listen to the podcast. Give the student a minute or two to read through the questions. You may make them short answer or multiple choice, depending on the level of your student.

For this particular podcast, I made them multiple choice, with less than 12 questions. You do not want to ask them too many questions. It will frustrate the student.

My multiple-choice questions required that they listen for intent as well as the basic information. I had the student listen to the podcast twice.

It is harder for them than the usual textbook, which has an accompanying audio component that is slow

142

with exact pronunciation that is very clear and easy to understand. On the other hand, the podcast is natural, with slang, not intentionally designed for ESL students.

After listening twice, the student compared the answers. This exercise really helped the student understand the content of the podcast. Then I listened again with the student, and focused on the points where the answers could be found.

Content. In this next section of the handout, the student has to think about the podcast overall (not individual questions) and answer this question: What is this radio program about?

Since the title of the worksheet was "Meeting New People Via Facebook," the student thought the answer was evident. But I gave the student a hint, telling him that the answer was not "socializing."

The student realized the deeper meaning of the podcast, that it was about illusion and reality in dating, not about socializing on facebook in general. This is a post-listening exercise.

Taking it with them

The tutor can use a podcast just as it is, getting the student involved in a simple discussion, however a handout, as above, focuses the students' attention.

After using your laptop computer to play the podcast, tell your student to take the podcast home with him or her. All they need is a USB storage device (a memory stick, an iPod, or a Walkman). They will have the handout and the media file so they can easily go over the lesson again at home.

Chapter 27

Getting To Know Each Other

A Lesson on Getting to Know Each Other

The tutor uses role-playing to help the student realize the correct words to use and the interplay of questions and responses, to get to know someone.

You can take turns role-playing the situation below with the student. Then the student can write about himself or herself. You can use that information to have a free form conversation with them.

Ultimately, in the future, the student can use these conversations as a model for real life conversations.

Getting To Know Each Other

What's your name?

My name is...

Where do you live?

I live in.............................Where were you born?

I was born in..

How many brothers and sisters do you have?

I   have..........................brother(s) and........................sister(s). .

Where did you go to school?

I went to ....

Are you married?

Yes, I am. / No, I'm not.

Do you have any children?

Yes, I have .... / No, I don't.

What do you do?

I work at a .... / I am a housewife. / I am a student.

What do you like to do?

I like to…………………………………………..……..

Meeting Someone for the First Time

A Hi, my name is………………………….

B Hello, I`m……………………Where are you from?

A I live in Nagoya. How about you?

B I live in Nagoya, too.

A Are you married?

B Yes, I am. (No, I`m not.)

A Do you have any children?

B Yes, I have two children. One daughter is ten and the other is five.

A Nice to meet you.

B Nice to meet you, too.

Chapter 28

Teaching Listening Skills

The purpose for teaching listening skills is for the student to recognize what they are actually hearing when they listen to English.

When the student first comes to this country and listens to people speaking English it doesn't make sense. It sounds like a bunch of jumbled sounds.

I understand this because I lived in Japan and that is how it was for me. It was very confusing and frustrating to learn Japanese by myself. It was impossible because when I heard a sound I could not associate it with a word or meaning. Eventually, I went to a Japanese tutor for help.

The tutor needs to help them make sense of these sounds, which is what we call listening exercises. The goal is for the student to be able to associate what they hear as a part of language and to also know what it means. For example, when they hear the word "cat" then they know it is a "c" sound followed by a soft "a" sound followed by a "t" sound. They also know that it refers to a small furry animal.

When teaching listening skills it is necessary to proceed slowly.

It requires playing short segments of the audio file, then stopping it and asking them to repeat the sounds, then rewinding it and playing it back.

The tutor identifies words the student doesn't understand and the sounds that he or she has trouble hearing. You can point out the word and its meaning. (Let them look it up in their electronic dictionary, if they want to.)

Teaching listening is a slow process; however it lays the groundwork for everything else. When a student can hear English well, then he or she can speak well and make a conversation well.

Hearing well means hearing each sound and being able to identify it. For example, when the student hears "cat" they can then write down the word, "C-A-T." He or she knows that the soft sound in between the c and t is the letter "a."

Sometimes, it is only possible to get through a couple sentences or one paragraph, depending upon the student's listening ability.

As a rule of thumb, if a student cannot understand your English very well during the tutoring session, they are not ready for an audio file.

In this case, you can teach them listening from speaking to them.

Speak using short, simple sentences.

Follow these steps:

1. Write each sentence down and speak it several times.

2. Have them speak it too.

(Note: When I tutor beginners, I only work with them for 30 minutes at a time. I ask them to bring a friend or relative that speaks English; and I write everything down. Usually they are really exhausted after 30 minutes. I also schedule multiple weekly sessions, 4 to 6 sessions per week. These beginners improve very rapidly. After a few months, I increase the lesson time to one hour two times a week.)

3. Take a simple conversation and read the parts back and forth.

4. Write up the conversation on paper and have the student follow along.

For example, you can read a conversation back and forth, where they are speaker A and you are speaker B, then switch back where you are speaker A and they are speaker B. Have them read the conversation on paper and follow along even when you are speaking.

You can write up your own simple little conversations or use conversations in a first level conversation book for ESL students.

Non-native speakers cannot hear English the same way we do.

It depends upon where they are from, what they can hear. For example, when a Japanese student hears the "e" sound they think it is an "i" because, in Japanese, an "i" sounds like an "e" sounds in English. I have listed some websites that have great audio files for download for ESL students.

6 minute English (BBC) –
http://www.bbc.co.uk/radio/podcasts/how2/

Real English (BBC) –
http://www.bbc.co.uk/radio/podcasts/re/

Talk About English (BBC) –
http://www.bbc.co.uk/radio/podcasts/tae/

Breaking News English podcasts-
http://www.breakingnewsenglish.com/podcast.html

ESL lab- http://www.esl-lab.com/guide.htm

http://www.wakeupenglish.com/free_dialogues/swf/dia
lma21.swf

BBC Radio program, law related news and free
podcasts/ downloads-
http://news.bbc.co.uk/1/hi/programmes/law_in_action/
default.stm (for native speakers and mainly about
Britain.)

http://www.wakeupenglish.com/free_dialogues/swf/dia
lma19.swf

A policeman asking questions about a robbery-
http://esl.about.com/library/listening/bllis_police.htm

Listen to this BBC Radio interview with Debra Veal-
http://www.bbc.co.uk/radio4/womanshour/2002_07_fri
_01.shtml

Chapter 29

Tips for Tutoring Adult Students

How do you effectively tutor English to an adult student who is struggling with English?

What will you actually do for 60 minutes together?

How will you make the lessons meaningful enough that your client feels satisfied and wants to retain you for future lessons?

First, you must know what the client wants and expects. Some tutors even present a written contract outlining their rates, the location and times of meetings, and payment policies.

I usually have very positive experiences with clients. I work with professionals, graduate students, and/or friends and spouses of friends. Be explicit about what you want and don't want to teach a client. Be prepared to provide policies for potential clients that you do not want to work with. For example, if you feel uncomfortable teaching the students at the lowest levels of English ability, you can decide that when they contact you on the phone. If they cannot communicate on the phone and need to have a friend call you, then you will not accept them as a client. You can politely tell the friend that you are not the best tutor to work with a beginning student.

For students who want to improve their conversation, you can choose materials ahead of time and email them to the student or give them the materials the lesson before, so they can prepare for the next lesson.

You can use newspapers and/or magazines to find appropriate articles to begin the conversation.

If you have a low level student wanting to improve their speaking skills, use a picture dictionary. You might use the Oxford Picture Dictionary to open conversations, and you can ask the student to bring in photographs each week. In addition, you can take old magazines to the lesson to use. You will need patience and be prepared to repeat words many times. Many students will want to work on their pronunciation. You can also ask/assign them listening activities on the web. You can ask lower level students to go to websites to practice their listening and speaking skills with drills.

You can earn an income helping ESL students write college admission essays, practice TOEFL and GRE essays, and proofreading papers. You can use the Cambridge Vocabulary in Use series and Grammar in Use series.

Chapter 30

ESL LESSONS: Utilizing Reading, Vocabulary and Speaking

Lesson 1 – Presidents and Other Men

The Story

The research scientist asked the president of the company if he could use his sick pay to attend his mother's funeral. There were only two months left in the year and he had never used his sick leave.

The president asked him to wait until after work that day while he considered the request.

The president then called the researcher back in and said, "If you are sick you can use your sick leave."

The next day the researcher called in sick and left town to attend his mother's funeral.

Vocabulary Practice

Mark the best choice.

'Leave' in this passage means…

a. going out of a building or room

b. a small green part of a tree

c. permission to be absent from work

d. asking someone for a favor

To 'attend' in this passage means to...

a. to pay for

b. to be present at

c. to observe

d. to avoid

Questions for Discussion

1. Why did the researcher go directly to the president to make the request?

2. Why did the researcher lie?

3. Would you lie in such a situation?

4. What would you think of a boss who would not let you attend your mother's funeral?

Activities

1. Use your own words to tell me the story.

2. Pronounce these words:

Research Scientist

President

Attend

Consider

Funeral

Lesson 2 – The Babysitter

The Story

While babysitting three children in an old house, I was laying on the sofa in my pajamas watching television. It was evening and I thought all the children were asleep upstairs. Suddenly, I was interrupted with loud screams from the kitchen. I ran out to the kitchen and saw the youngest child standing with the refrigerator door open. The pitcher was on the floor on its side. There was liquid all over the floor. The child was screaming. I grabbed the pitcher off the floor and, when I turned around, the small child had run out the back kitchen door. I ran out to fetch him and when I returned and tried to open the door it was locked. I crept around the house, stopping to fumble with windows. They were all secured tightly. I heard laughing. I looked up to the second floor window where the two older children were watching me.

Vocabulary Practice

Mark the best choice.

Interrupted' means…

a. introduced to someone new

b. avoided

c. to move from one place to another

d. to stop what you are doing because of something else

The word 'crept' means to…

a. move quickly

b. leap up and down

c. crawl on your hands and knees

d. move quietly

To fumble means to…

a. handle an object confidently

b. break an object

c. to handle an object awkwardly

d. pound on an object

A 'pitcher' is a…

a. glass

b. bottle of milk

c. glass container for liquids

d. a large bowl

Questions for Discussion

1. What is funny about the story?

2. What is dramatic about the story?

3. Why did the babysitter go outside?

4. What do you think will happen next?

Activities

1. Tell me the story using your own words.

2. Pronounce these words:

Babysitter

Pitcher

Crept

Fumble

Fetch

Secured

Tightly

Lesson 3 – Trouble Comes in Twos

The Story

The student was exiting the coffee shop when she was approached by two beggars outside. "So, you're operating in twos now?"

"No," one of them replied. "While I ask you for money, the other guy grabs your purse and runs with it."

Vocabulary Practice

Mark the best choice.

A 'beggar' is…

a. a person who gives things away

b. a person who has no money

c. a person who asks for money

d. a person who offers to work for money

"Operating" in this case, means...

a. to approach people kindly

b. to speak loudly

c. to operate on a patient

d. doing something illegally

When a person is "approached" they are...

a. looked at

b. harassed

c. attacked

d. spoken to by others

The word 'grabs' used in this passage means ....

a. borrows

b. helps you carry something

c. offers to help you

d. steals

Questions for Discussion

1. What is this joke telling us about beggars?

2. What is the difference between a beggar and a thief?

Activities

1. Tell me the story using your own words.

2. Pronounce these words:

Beggar

Approached

Replied

Grab

How does this proverb apply to this story(joke)?

A man is known by the company he keeps

Chapter 31

Great Websites with Free ESL Lessons

The Internet TESL Journal

The Internet TESL Journal is my favorite website for teaching and tutoring in ESL. It has lessons and tips on teaching and tutoring. I will list below the abstracts for a few applicable articles in the journal that apply to tutoring as well as one article I published. If you want to read the full articles, you can go to their website.

http://iteslj.org/

How to Use Skype in the ESL/EFL Classroom

Sarah Elaine Eaton

This paper discusses how Skype can be used to: 1) empower ESL/EFL teachers and tutors to incorporate a simple and popular technology into their teaching practice 2) give presentations and workshops 3) be a stepping stone to using more sophisticated technology in the classroom. For those who are new to using technology in the language learning classroom, Skype is an effective way to experiment while minimizing the risk of things going wrong. Skype can help ESL/EFL teachers improve their technology literacy and increase their confidence using technology in the classroom. It provides an excellent stepping stone for those who are not entirely "fluent" with more sophisticated technologies. This paper builds upon previous work done on using Skype for literacy and language learning (Eaton, 2009a, 2010c).

Teaching Speaking: Activities to Promote Speaking in a Second Language

Hayriye Kayi

Speaking is a critical part of second language learning and teaching. However, even though we all know it is very important, for many years, teaching speaking skills have focused on speaking in the form of a drill or memorization of dialogue. However, in order to live in the world, we now realize that the goal of teaching speaking needs to improve the students' communicative skills. In order to help people improve their speaking, some speaking activities are provided in Hayriye Kayi's article.

Using Pictures from Magazines

Joep van der Werff

In Joep van der Werff's article, he shows how pictures from magazines can be used for teaching international people how to speak English. Through using magazine articles, the teacher can assign activities in all of the areas, such as, speaking, listening, writing, vocabulary and grammar. The author gives tips on how to obtain and arrange good pictures. He also includes several sample activities. Teachers or tutors can use the activities as they are presented, or adapt them to fit their needs.

Teaching *The Three Little Pigs* to EFL Young Learners in Taiwan

Su-Yueh Wu

In this article, the author, Su-Yueh Wu, shows how picture books can be used as an effective aid for learning English. The main purpose of the paper is to show how young learners in Taiwan learned English by using folktales in picture books. The author of this article shows several teaching techniques, such as, presenting the picture book, using flash cards, showing sentence stripes, playing puppets for story drama, playing the chosen story CD, reading aloud, role play, choral speaking/chanting, and singing songs with action. The finding of this author's research showed that the use of multiple teaching techniques in teaching this folktale had strong effect on increasing the young learners' English listening and speaking performance.

Teacher-made Activities for a Computer-based ESL/EFL Class

Anil Pathak

The author of this article explains how computer-based classes are increasing. More teachers are using commercially available software to teach ESL. But it isn't very good because it focuses on the student learning alone not on an online classroom. The author of this article shows how teachers can integrate their own curriculum materials into the computer based classroom so that it is more applicable for their students. The author provides three examples of activities. The activities use simple and commonly used software such as Microsoft Power Point and Microsoft Word. Also, they are sufficiently open for teachers to modify them according to their objectives.

The Talking Stick: An American Indian Tradition in the ESL Classroom

Kimberly Fujioka
kimberlyfujioka [AT] yahoo.com
"...to begin always anew, to make, to reconstruct, and not to spoil, to refuse to bureaucratize the mind, to

understand and to live life as a process--live to become..."Paulo Freire

Introduction

In this paper, I will overview the scholarship which calls for a more democratic teaching practice in the classroom. Secondly, "The Talking Stick", will be introduced as a listening and speaking methodology that is "transformative" and serves as a bridge to cross-cultural understanding in the ESL classroom. Teaching practice is described, in detail, with Asian university students. In the final section, the author offers suggestions to teachers about when to use the talking stick method and how to use this method with students who have different English usage abilities.

Scholarship in Pedagogy

Traditional teaching practice places the professor in the front of the classroom and the students assembled in rows of desks, all facing the chalkboard. The unchallenged assumption underlying this set-up, is that the teacher has knowledge that the students want to get. The students memorize information, provided by the teacher through lectures, and at a later time, reproduce it in some kind of examination. The problem with this traditional pedagogy is that students do not become actively involved in the learning process. They think of themselves as passive consumers of education, where information, not true knowledge, becomes just another thing to buy. Paulo Freire (1976) refers to this as "the banking system of education" where the students are seen as passive consumers.

In these traditional ways of teaching students feel left out of the process. Students have reported to me that in their other classes, where the traditional style of teaching is used, they feel tired and bored, and, they say they feel like their presence is not needed.

The need to change our teaching style, to incorporate more democratic methods which would reflect the multicultural classroom in ESL teaching, is especially necessary, where the use of English is critical to the learning process. Since the late 1980's much research has been done in language learning, which suggests a move toward a more learner-centered approach. The contributors of the scholarship in this vein, have described it as a more communicative approach to language learning. Nunan (1988) stresses the necessity of the teacher "doing things with language as opposed to learning about language", while Di Pietro (1987) addresses the motivational factors involved in language learning by suggesting students choose their own topics. Some scholarship has also stressed the influence of culture on the interpretation of the meaning of words (Wolfson, 1988), reminding us of the sociolinguistic elements of language, which must also be taken into consideration in the way a teacher approaches the subject. The point being, the teaching style is critical to whether students learn language or not, and this style is influenced by culture, politics, social class and gender issues. In this sense, the "how" of teaching must reflect that multicultural world in which we live. Bell Hooks' transformative teaching is an example of a teaching style which is based on an awareness of the differences which exist in our world, and contains a basic respect for multiculturalism. Hooks describes her teaching practice:

In the classroom setting that I have witnessed the power of transformative pedagogy rooted in a respect for multiculturalism. Working with a critical pedagogy based on my understanding of Freire's teaching, I enter the classroom with the assumption that we must build 'community' in order to create a climate of openness and intellectual rigor. Rather than focusing on issues of safety, I think that a feeling of community creates a sense that there is a shared commitment and common good that binds us. What we all ideally share is the desire to learn--to receive actively knowledge that enhances our intellectual development and our capacity to live more fully in the world. (Hooks, pg. 40)

The aims of democracy, as a yardstick for evaluating pedagogy, has been acknowledged more recently, especially in the work of Paulo Freire, who led the way, in the late 1970's with his work in education "as the practice of freedom". (Freire, 1976) Education can be a way for people to learn to question, says Freire (Freire, 1989), and, as a result, for people to become more free. Freire advises teachers to learn how to teach by observing student's learning styles, and developing teaching methods based on that.(Freire, 1998). Mark Gerzon, in his "Teaching Democracy by Doing it", suggests an entire curriculum based on a more democratic pedagogical style (Gerzon, 1997). The Talking Stick is a listening and speaking method in language learning, which is democratic and encourages understanding between students from culturally diverse backgrounds. This method incorporates an open style of listening, within a space of silence.

The Talking Stick is based on Native American Tradition

The Talking Stick was a method used by native Americans, to let everyone speak their mind during a council meeting, a type of tribal meeting. According to the indigenous American's tradition, the stick was imbued with spiritual qualities, that called up the spirit of their ancestors to guide them in making good decisions. The stick ensured that all members, who wished to speak, had their ideas heard. All members of the circle were valued equally.

Dr. Locust, at the American Research and Training Center in Tucson, Arizona, describes the talking stick, according to native American tradition:

"The talking stick has been used for centuries by many Indian tribes as a means of just and impartial hearing. The talking stick was commonly used in council circles to decide who had the right to speak. When matters of great concern would come before the council, the leading elder would hold the talking stick, and begin the discussion. When he would finish what he had to say, he would hold out the talking stick, and whoever would speak after him would take it. In this manner, the stick would be passed from one individual to another until all who wanted to speak had done so. The stick was then passed back to the elder for safe keeping." (Locust, 1998)

168

Talking Stick Rules

There are rules about using the talking stick, which Locust states:

"Whoever holds the talking stick has within his hands the power of words. Only he can speak while he holds the stick, and the other council members must remain silent. The eagle feather tied to the stick gives him the courage and wisdom to speak truthfully and wisely. The rabbit fur on the end of the stick, reminds him that his words must come from his heart. " (Locust, 1998)

We all know that speaking the truth is powerful. The history of AA (Alcoholic Anonymous) and other step programs and the practice of psychotherapy are all based on this awareness: that speaking the truth is healing. But it is healing for the group as a whole because as each individual listens, in silence and reverence, a whole world of understanding opens up.

When to use the Talking Stick

I ask the students to move their chairs into a circle. In my class, I have the students imagine that they are holding a stick. Whoever is holding the stick is asked to speak from his heart on the subject or issue in question. The other students are not to speak but also they are not to think ahead, about what they are going to say. They are supposed to let themselves concentrate on the words of the speaker, seeking to understand. When it is their turn to speak, they can trust that the "right" words will come. This assures that everyone is heard. That is the most important point.

First, we must all listen. The setting is non-judgmental. Whatever the student's viewpoint, that is okay. No one is allowed to comment on what another has said. This method, I have observed in many classes, will yield new awareness and insights.

After all the students spoke, and rested over the weekend, and we returned to class the next week, the issue was seen in a much more holistic way.

From my observations, no one had the desire to cling to their former notions on what should be done to stop opium production and the end to drug use in the world. What was achieved was a deeper understanding of the situation, and a mutual respect for each other based on "really listening".

After the passing of The Talking Stick, my students often say that they felt really "heard" by the others, and that they felt the others understood them, within their own cultural framework. Most importantly, they heard themselves. Their experience was affirmed in an academic setting; and they experienced a real transformation in the classroom. In short, the insights they experienced were not only for in the classroom, but could be applied to their everyday lives.

Implications for Teaching

Use this method when you want the students to listen to others as part of a learner-centered curriculum. This method takes the focus off the teacher, as the sole purveyor of knowledge. And by using it, students are encouraged to learn from each other.

The teacher can provide language materials with simple, everyday dialog and situations, whereby the students can role-play the parts while in possession of the talking stick. (Who decides who is to hold the stick, and when?) Begin with one assigned student, who then chooses another student to pass the talking stick to, and so on. The others listen attentively because they do not know if they will be passed the talking stick next.

For more advanced language users, topic or issue-based content material is excellent because it gives them content they can get excited about, and issues they can address with passion. The teacher can start by presenting on the overhead projector, a newspaper article that addresses an important issue, for example, violence in the schools. The teacher should use a real news story which presents a detailed situation. When each student is in possession of the stick, he or she is asked to speak whatever comes to their mind on the topic. The others are to listen with an open mind; and with no self-rehearsal going on in their minds, concerning what they will say. Then the next student speaks and so on.

Conclusion

As language teachers, the way we teach communicates a lot to students; it says who we are and what we believe. Our pedagogical style and teaching methods can build a bridge to a sharing of meaning between people from very different cultural backgrounds. In our multicultural classrooms, there is a lot we can learn from the students as well. We are all victims of our own culturally limited perspectives, if we let ourselves. If we are open to see things from another point-of-view, we can grow. As a world, people from all nations--the developed western countries and the developing countries--need to listen to each other with an open heart, to arrive at a kind of mutual understanding that we so desperately need to solve today's global problems. Teaching methods in today's global environment need to be flexible enough to acknowledge the student's cultural and individual differences, in an accepting and open-hearted atmosphere. The Talking Stick is an example of one of these methods.

The Internet TESL Journal, Vol. IV, No. 9,
September 1998
http://iteslj.org/

I have published a number of articles on the Internet TESL Journal. You can look up my name to see the other articles and lesson plans I have published.

II. Dave Sperling's ESL Café

Dave Sperling's ESL Café is another one of my favorite sites. Dave has been teaching ESL for years and has thousands of teaching ideas, lessons and tips on his site. Here is the web address for grammar lessons. I suggest when tutoring to scroll down to the "Conversational Grammar" lessons. These are the most interesting and applicable to the tutoring situation. http://www.eslcafe.com/

Chapter 32

Shopping Lesson Plan

This is a sample shopping lesson plan. You can use this lesson as a way to introduce the student to shopping. You can show them the correct words to use and let them practice with you. You can even take them on a field trip where they can use English to shop, with you guiding them.

Shopping

The store clerk:

May I help you? / Can I help you?

Are you looking for something?

What size?

Cash or charge?

Have a nice day!

The customer:

I`m looking for a summer sweater.

Where are the shoes?

Do you have winter coats?

How much is this?

Do you have this in size seven?

Money:

bills, coins, cash, personal check, charge card, plastic money, traveler`s checks,

100 cents (¢) = 1 dollar ($)

$ .25 twenty-five cents a quarter

$ .99 ninety-nine cents

$ 2.50 two dollars and fifty cents two and a half dollars

$ 89.99 eighty-nine dollars and ninety-nine cents

In a Supermarket

A Do you have rice?

B Yes, we do. It's here.

A Where are the soft drinks?

B Over there.

A Thanks.

In a Convenience Store

A How much is this ice cream?

B It`s $ .75.

A Do you have chocolate?

B Sorry, we only have vanilla.

A OK. I will take two.

In a Shoe Store

A Can I help you?

B Yes, I'm looking for some jogging shoes.

A What color?

B White.

A What size?

B Seven and a half.

A Just a minute..................... Please try them on.

B They're just right. How much are they?

A They're $69.99.

B I'll take them.

A Cash or charge?

B Traveler's checks.

Chapter 33

ESL Lessons Using Newspaper Articles

Newspaper articles have been used by ESL instructors for years because we know that students enjoy reading news. The information is current and is relevant to the student's everyday lives. In addition, students want to know the culture of living in America, so they can feel part of society. Through news stories new immigrants and international students can understand a lot about the American culture.

Studies in ESL have shown that when study materials have compelling and relevant content, students are willing to do the extra work, such as look up words they don't know, in order to understand the assignment. In turn, these news stories can be used to stimulate general conversations which ESL students need to engage in, to develop their speaking skills.

The following news stories were rewritten by me, based on actual news clips. You can rewrite simple news stories from your local newspaper for your own students. Use stories that are short, that is, only a few paragraphs and have interesting but not disturbing content. Disturbing content could mean sexually explicit content, prejudicial content or overly political content. You will have to use your judgment on this depending upon knowing your student.

Note: As a suggestion, based upon my 25 years of tutoring, I would advise you to keep every story you rewrite, along with the questions. You can later compile your news stories and use them with other students. Over time these news stories will become more valuable.

Scientific Research Shows the Stomach has Bacteria that Divides all People into Three Basic Types

As early as the 1900s it was discovered by scientists that there were a total of only four blood types by which all human beings can be classified. Recently scientists have discovered that there are only three ecosystems within the stomach for all human beings. These ecosystems in the stomach consist of microbes, bacteria and enzymes. Each ecosystem type has different health consequences because of the different combinations of microbes and bacteria that help digest food and absorb vitamins.

Scientists have tried to find out who has the different ecosystem. Some of the questions they ask are as follows. Do people of the same ethnic background have the same ecosystem? Their answer is no. These scientists also tried to find out if these different ecosystems can be similar in people who are of the same sex or weight. The answer is no. Other explanations are being studied. Currently this is not known but is being studied diligently.

Why is this important? When scientists discover who has the different ecosystem type, they can predict health problems and advise doctors on how to treat patients based upon their own type. For example, people who are of Type I create more enzymes for making vitamin B7 but Type 2 people make more enzymes that create vitamin B1. People who are Type I have more vitamin B7, naturally, but less vitamin B1. These deficiencies can lead to medical problems. Therefore, doctors would be able to understand a patient's medical problems better when they know their ecosystem type.

In the future, when we go to the doctor, we will be tested for our ecosystem type, or the naturally occurring enzymes and bacteria in our stomach. We will be classified as Type I, 2 or 3. Doctors will be better able to treat us as patients by knowing this important information.

Vocabulary:

Stomach

Bacteria

Ecosystems

Classified

Scientific

Research

Diligently

Deficiencies

Enzymes

Microbe

Predict

Advise

This rewritten article is based on a news clip from the *New York Times* by Carl Zimmer entitled, "Gut Bacteria Divide People into 3 Types, Scientists Report" April 20, 2011.

Questions

What makes up the ecosystem in the stomach?

a. bacteria

b. microbes and bacteria

c. microbes

Do all people have the same ecosystem in their stomach?

a. Yes

b. no

Microbes and bacteria in the stomach…

a. help people digest food.

b. help people absorb vitamins.

c. both a and b.

Why is it important for scientists to know the ecosystem in the stomach?

a. To predict health problems

b. To advise doctors on how to treat patients.

c. Both a and b.

Questions that require verbal responses

Why are bacteria and microbes good?

What is your blood type?

Discussion for more advanced speakers

When you go to the doctor what do you say?

Role play

Pretend you are the doctor and the student comes to your office to report a problem.

Procedure for helping ESL students learn English from the Newspaper

1. Do the first lesson during the class time so that you can show the student what to do.(After the first lesson, you just give the student this as a take home assignment. They will take home the news story with the vocabulary and the questions and do them at home. The next class time they will bring the homework to the lesson and you will go over it with them. You can also do the verbal questions during the lesson time and engage the student in a conversation about the news story.)

2. Give them the vocabulary words first and have them look up the words they don't understand in the dictionary. They should write down the definitions.

3. Ask the student to read the news story.

4. Ask the student if he or she understands the story. If he says no, then ask him what he doesn't understand. This may require him to look up words in his own translation or electronic dictionary.

This may require you to explain some word or concept meanings to him.

5. Ask the student to answer the questions.

6. Ask the student to answer the verbal questions.

7. Engage the student in a conversation about the news story based on the questions you have written.

8. If the student is able to successfully complete all 7 steps above, ask them to write a paragraph describing what they have read.

The lessons using a newspaper story are mostly for intermediate level to high level ESL students. In other words, if a student cannot make a simple conversation with you during the lesson, then they are not ready to do a lesson using a newspaper article. However, for students who can make a basic conversation with you, this type of lesson is excellent practice for them to enter into more challenging conversations based upon content.

For example, many high school students from other countries have come to me saying that they cannot engage in classroom discussions because they are not confident about their English usage ability. In fact, they cannot discuss topics in the classroom for a number of reasons: the classroom participation is fast and they cannot use English that quickly. In addition, the classroom is comprised of native speakers of English who use difficult words that they do not understand.

When you, as their tutor, do the newspaper story lesson with them, they can improve their skills that will help them engage in classroom conversations and or debates.

Note: as a student improves their ability to read, you can skip the step where you have to rewrite the news clip. You can just give them a news clip from the local newspaper for homework with your questions. In addition, a student may request news stories in a particular subject area. A student may request longer articles such as magazine articles. In this case you can find many magazine articles online and print them out for the student. In short, as students improve they will need longer and more difficult pieces. However it will be easier for you, as the tutor, because you won't have to rewrite stories and the conversations will be more engaging and enjoyable.

Appendix

Where to Post Your Online Tutoring Service

Most students enrolling in online ESL classes want specific language instruction that targets their problem areas - such as speaking, grammar or writing skills.

A few good sites where ESL tutors can find work includes ESLTeachersBoard, findateacher, and Europa. Do a google search and look up: Find An Online ESL Language Tutor or Find Work As a Tutor to locate companies that employ people to work as an online tutors.

Definitions of Curriculum Terms

Survival Skills. The English skills needed to function in everyday life are survival skills. These skills are categorized at different levels from 1 to 6, so teachers can identify students by level and then teach them accordingly. If a student functions at a level one then the goal is to help them to improve their skills to reach level two. These skills are just a guide to identify where a student is in their skills level and to monitor their improvement. Thanks to Megan Esler from Portland Community College in 1982 who developed these skill sets.

Grammar. Grammar is the formal structure of language, that is, how it works. Some students have been formally educated in English grammar while others simply have learned grammar indirectly. It is not necessary to teach grammar directly in order for ESL students to improve their conversation skills. However, indirectly the tutor must let them know if they are using English in a grammatically incorrect way, and then modify their usage, in order to speak English well.

Fluency. Fluency is how well the student communicates their ideas using language. Fluency is what we strive for in teaching ESL. What that means is this: we do not expect the student to speak like a native born American. We help them improve their ability to use English to communicate and to survive in this world.

Vocabulary. To teach new words and to review old vocabulary. All ESL students need to continually learn new vocabulary in order to improve their ability to use English.

Literacy. The ability to read and understand language. Ask the student if they can use another language. If they can use, for example, Japanese then they are literate but not in English. This means that they have the ability to learn English because you know they have already mastered their first language.

Pronunciation. The sounds of the language as they are used in sentences and in words. Pronunciation problems may result in the student having trouble making the correct sounds. It may also result in putting stress on the wrong places within a word or in a sentence.

Non-verbal Communication. The communication we use everyday that does not require words, such as, facial expressions, hand gestures, tone of voice, loudness of voice, and posturing, the way a person stands or acts.

Teaching Style. Teaching Style refers to the way you help your students learn English. Some examples are: through conversation, vocabulary building, role playing where you help the student use language by reading a script and having them play a role as a way to learn the appropriate words to say in a special situation. Another teaching technique is using audio tapes or podcasts for students to listen to as part of the lesson. This audio helps the students learn to hear English so they can listen more accurately in everyday life.

About the Author

Kimberly Fujioka taught English as a Second Language, at the university level, from 1982 to 2010. She received her BA in Psychology/English from the University of Pennsylvania in 1982. She studied for her first graduate degree in English Literature in 1983 at Duquesne University in Pittsburgh, Pennsylvania. In 2000 she completed a graduate degree, in Applied Linguistics (Teaching English as a Second Language) at the University of Surrey. She has tutored hundreds of students in English as a Second Language since 1982.

Kimberly has written and published numerous professional papers in the field of Applied Linguistics and several chapters in published books, including To Japan with Love: A Travel Guide for the Connoisseur (2009) and Saturdays with Lillian (2010).

She has written and published many short stories and poetry in literary journals. Kimberly currently works as an editor at the business she founded in 2004, **English Writing Help, Inc.** which specializes in editing books and academic and scientific writing for professional researchers. The website is: http://www.englishwritinghelp.com

English Writing Help, Inc.

Kimberly lives in Honolulu with her husband and son.